Jerusalem Diary:
Searching for the Tomb
and House of Jesus

JOANNA KUJAWA Ph.D.

BALBOA.
PRESS

A DIVISION OF HAY HOUSE

Balboa Press books may be ordered through booksellers or by contacting:

Balboa Press
A Division of Hay House
1663 Liberty Drive
Bloomington, IN 47403
www.balboapress.com.au
1-(877) 407-4847

ISBN: 978-1-4525-0637-1 (sc)
ISBN: 978-1-4525-0638-8 (e)

Library of Congress Control Number: 2012913264

Because of the dynamic nature of the Internet, any web addresses or links contained in this book may have changed since publication and may no longer be valid. The views expressed in this work are solely those of the author and do not necessarily reflect the views of the publisher, and the publisher hereby disclaims any responsibility for them.

The author of this book does not dispense medical advice or prescribe the use of any technique as a form of treatment for physical, emotional, or medical problems without the advice of a physician, either directly or indirectly. The intent of the author is only to offer information of a general nature to help you in your quest for emotional and spiritual well-being. In the event you use any of the information in this book for yourself, which is your constitutional right, the author and the publisher assume no responsibility for your actions.

Cover Art by John Hicks, Getty Images
Also published by Sail Media 12/2009

Printed in the United States of America

Balboa Press rev. date: 08/03/2012

CONTENTS

DEDICATION

I offer this book to all seekers. This book is not about answers or truth. It is a book about a personal journey. The journey began when Steve and Martin, my travelling companions, decided to share with me their archaeological discoveries of what they believed to be Jesus' house in Nazareth and his tomb in Jerusalem. When they first told me, my whole being caught fire—an unexpected reaction for me—a lapsed catholic for many years who now took more interest in meditation than any form of Christianity. My reaction told me that I would be going on an unforgettable spiritual adventure. I can now admit that the journey has been, at times, outrageous, tragi-comic, and perhaps even controversial. Yet the purpose of this book is not to create controversy, but rather to look at the old traditions with an innocent eye, unpolluted by old convictions, fears and loyalties. And even more so, to encourage openness to alternative interpretations and visions. Undoubtedly, all old religious traditions have great truths in them. But I believe some of these truths were interpreted in the spirit of the times in which they were pronounced, and are thus limited. I often wonder if the great individuals around whom old religions were built would recognise their words as they are being taught now. Truth might be one, but our understanding of it might be different. What our predecessors were not ready to accept, we might. So I invite you to join me on my journey on searching for Yeshua, a misunderstood Teacher, hidden behind traditional dogmas.

I would like to thank all the scholars and enlightened beings whom I have had the chance to encounter in person or through literature. Here I would especially like to mention my guru, Swamiji, scholars from the University of Toronto, Coleman Barks and his amazing translations of Rumi, the translators and interpreters of the Gnostic Gospels (of Mary Magdalene, Thomas, and Philip), as well as Peter Brown and J. N. D. Kelly, biographers of great, controversial saints such as Augustine of Hippo and Jerome. Finally, I thank Steve and Martin, my two companions on this journey. I would also like to thank everyone who crossed our path in Israel/Palestine and/or who reads this book.

In the spirit of great gratitude and adventure, I give this book to you.

PROLOGUE

I am in the Seven Arches Hotel on the Mount of Olives. I open the door to my room, drop my purse on the grey carpeted floor and am drawn to the view from the window. The temples of Jerusalem, strangely seductive, are looking back at me like floating lights in the serene black sky. I pull a chair over to the window and collapse into it in a long, deep sleep.

At 4.45 am, still seated at the window, the call from the mosque awakes me. The sky above the mad holy city has changed: the navy blue darkness is transformed into a paler, subtler blue—as beautiful and unusual as the city below. From my window I can see the medieval wall surrounding the Old City, with the Golden Dome of the Rock Mosque at its heart. Far behind the innumerable lines of winding streets, I search for the black roofs of the Holy Sepulchre which was once the symbol of Christian presence there. This is the city in which the Crusaders slaughtered Jews and Moslems alike in the name of Christ. Then, in turn, the Islamic kings slaughtered the Crusaders, whom they saw as hordes of 'infidels'. I look out the window and I breathe with awe and horror. In an eternal city like this one nothing changes. Now it is a city in which the Palestinians are like despairing lovers, not allowed to claim their parts of their Beloved, where the Zionists are like jealous spouses, unwilling to share what they believe to be only theirs, and where the Christians, bewildered by TV preachers, try to retrace the steps of their strangely vulnerable God. Human passions are always complicated and strained. If there is one relationship in human life that can rise beyond the complexities of fear and anger, it is our relationship with God. But not in Jerusalem, the city of great passions.

I am in the dark night of the soul, I write in my diary while sitting by my window in the Seven Arches Hotel. *If only I knew what was going on with me.* I beg my mind for answers, but it cannot give me any. Yet my state of mind is not uncommon. The mystics talk of this as the 'dark night of the soul'—a time where you lose sight of your ultimate goals and can see nothing ahead. A time in your life when your ego breaks down, leading to a complete collapse of everything that has been important to you, everything that you believed defined you, everything that has brought you a sense of status, self-value and identity. The end of your personal world. You don't understand what has happened or why. Haven't you done everything right? You check your mental notes against the wisdom of the world, and everything you were taught *was* right. Yes, you conclude, you have done everything right. You have worked hard towards your goals. You have achieved them, but are left with no praise, no rewards, no pat on the shoulder. Just dust in your mouth. And if you have faith, that faith is being tested since, according to all worldly signs, God has forgotten you too. So, yes, the great mystics write about a 'dark ecstasy', when what you know as the 'truth' is exposed as delusion and destroyed. Somewhere along the way, much later, you learn that this breakdown in misconceptions about yourself and the world can be transformed so a deeper vision and wisdom can nestle in our hearts. I wish I could say this transformation had happened blissfully; in my case it was more like a hurricane.

For a moment I sit quietly by the window with my diary on my lap before the day begins, as Jerusalem becomes temporarily silent after the call from the mosque. The next sound, of distant bells, falls upon the city at exactly 6.13 am. At 7.25 am the moon moves right above the Golden Dome in the full light of the day. I want to discover and embrace the whole of the city. Right now. At this very moment. Without waiting or delay. To walk the streets of the city, looking for traces of the man whose image terrified me in my childhood. The strange, sad man with bleeding face and tormented body. The English translation of his name would probably be Joshua. In Aramaic, the language he spoke, it was Yeshua. This was the name his mother called him—the name Mary Magdalene called him. His teachings became so obscured that, in time, what was left of them were a few enigmatic stories and a new Latinised version of his name— *Jesus.* I want to strip him of the layers of tales and images I was fed as a child in religious classes, and meet the young man, the inspiring teacher, rebellious rabbi and great spiritual being. In Jerusalem. In the Seven Arches Hotel, room 301.

HOUSE OF A TRAVELLER

'This is the key', the woman said. She was tall and dressed in black, with a touch of the gothic. 'I don't think he uses any of that much.' She looked around. 'Nice place, actually.'

We were in Richmond, Melbourne, and the woman was handing me over the keys so I could house-sit, or rather, have a place to live, until I sorted out my mess. The moody, rainy day fitted my state of mind well.

I looked around. The place was spacious and nearly empty; there was a certain hollowness about it—a feeling that no one had really lived here.

'He's hardly here', the woman said. 'He's a traveller.'

'A traveller? Where does he travel?'

'Mostly Jerusalem and Cyprus, I think.'

I took the key from her and dropped my suitcases. There were still some boxes of books waiting for me in front of the house. *Traveller? One traveller sitting a house for another.* I walked from room to room and decided to settle into the studio at the back of the house, regardless of whether or not he might agree to rent it to me later. The walls were empty and I was disappointed to see there were no books in the house—or so it appeared at first. Books are the soul of every traveller's home,

1

however fleeting their stay. I knew the tension of the freedom between travel and adventure and the desire to belong and have a room of one's own. The tension every traveller lives. 'When I have my own space again', I thought, 'I'll give it more life—like the places I had in Toronto and Kuala Lumpur'. I unrolled my Mexican rug with its Aztec Warrior (to give me strength and courage) onto the floor and on the empty shelves I placed a few pictures from Canada, Cambodia and Malaysia (to give me some continuity), along with my Guru's books (to give me guidance) and meditation CDs (to help me find a way to Bliss again). These were all both valuables and possessions.

I went into Steve's storage room. Maybe it wasn't my business, but I couldn't help myself. I was too curious about him now. Earlier, on the kitchen counter I found a photo of a tall man snooping among some ancient ruins somewhere. That photo spoke to a forgotten part of me that had dreamt of exotic adventures. I was fascinated by this man I had never met before. 'It must be him', I thought. Lying on the floor were stacks of books: *The Gospel of Mary Magdalene, The Gospel of Thomas, The Gospel of Judas, The Urantia Book*. I dusted off the covers as I browsed through the familiar pages.

In my twenties I studied such things. When I was six my mother took me for a walk to a university and said, 'One day you will study here'. Her statement could have had something to do with the fact I was brought up in Poland during the worst political and economic crisis in Eastern Europe. Back then there were only two choices: either you became a drunk (even in a crisis there was still plenty of vodka for desperate workers in a communist state), or you became an intellectual (even in the worst crises, you could go to the libraries and read philosophers—especially if they had been dead for a long time

2

and hadn't had the chance to contradict Karl Marx). I decided that being an intellectual was the better choice, since I had never had a head strong enough for straight shots of vodka. So I went on to university to study philosophy. Sometimes I think this was a gift. It depends on the point of view, you see. In Poland there were no distractions, no drugs—only a black and white television with two channels. Which was just as well—I became a philosopher and a writer. I was especially drawn to medieval philosophy and history, which was as far from the morbid form of Eastern European Marxism as I could imagine. Shortly after I began my studies in Poland I left for Paris and then Canada, where I gained a prestigious scholarship from the University of Toronto to study esoteric medieval philosophy texts. But life is never that simple. Underneath my scholarly explorations I secretly dreamed of exotic adventures.

'Mostly Jerusalem and Cyprus.' I thought of Steve the traveller as I was browsing through his books. 'He sounds like a medieval pilgrim.' And I left it at that for now.

I soon sank back into panic and anxiety. On the tram to Chapel Street I looked through the unemployment assistance forms, feeling sick in my stomach. The tram passed by apartments on the Yarra River and slowly moved on to boutiques on Chapel Street. The closer we got to High Street, the more my feelings of nausea increased. By the time I had joined the queue for the unemployed I was feeling faint.

'How much did you earn in the last fortnight?' the woman at the counter asked a tired-looking man in a worn-out blue jumper who was handing her his form. 'A hundred and ten dollars? We have a report from your employer that you earned a hundred and ten dollars and eighty-five cents!' she exclaimed triumphantly. 'That's called falsifying records.'

The man in the blue jumper cringed and tried to explain himself to the woman, but she didn't look appeased. He shrank a little more, then more again, until he almost disappeared under the counter. The woman stamped his form with a warning; the man sighed with relief and thanked her profusely. At that moment I wished I was a samurai and could cut her head off with one precise move.

I crossed the street and waited for a tram. Chapel Street, usually so lively, was soaked in a grey rain. Young men walking down the street looked shabby and wasted. Or maybe it was me? I saw my reflection in the pharmacy window, my wild hair caught by the wind and the rain—I looked like a blond medusa on a bad day. I had no umbrella with me and stood there by the window thinking, 'So this is where twenty years of education and travel has brought me?' A great wave of despair was building up in my belly, like a persistent, sickening feeling.

My mind was racing back to my past. *What has gone wrong?* Until recently, things had always been falling into place. After I received my degrees in Toronto, I was asked to teach at an Australian university in Kuala Lumpur and then to finish a Ph.D in Melbourne. The scholarships ended with the Ph.D, which I expected, but the jobs I had believed would become available to me never materialised. Suddenly, all the doors had closed. People whom I used to work with and who could have helped me get a job again were moved away from my path. Consumed by my studies, I did not know they had fallen into disgrace; even mentioning their names on my CV was an act of self-defeat. In the end, I managed to get three hours tutoring a subject in which I had previously lectured and developed. I could have got another three in another department, but the dragon lady in administration decided it was not desirable for one tutor to work in two separate departments. 'I have no money to pay my rent', I begged her to no avail as she enjoyed her superiority behind her desk. For a while I stayed afloat by taking care of an elderly person until, through a friend, I had learned about the possibility of house-sitting Steve's house and perhaps, after he returned, staying in the studio at the back. That solved my rent money issues for now.

By the time the tram finally arrived I was soaking wet and looking less like a medusa and more like a wet fish, my hair sticking to my head like disjointed fins. I hopped onto the tram enthusiastically. Five minutes into the trip I realised I was going in the wrong direction.

About two and a half weeks later, Steve returned. He met me in the studio. Tall, grey-haired and eagle-like, he moved with self-conscious precision. His world appeared to be as much in control as mine was spiralling into chaos. He looked a little tired, unfocused, when he asked me to join him for a cup of tea. I had the impression he didn't really care where he was or who he was going to talk with.

We were sitting in his garden at a round white table with a pot of tea, two mugs and some biscuits; the evening was falling softly on Richmond and the light was caught in the moment between reddish haze of afternoon and the early summer night. I smelled the subtle scent of violet bells growing wild in his otherwise well-trimmed garden. Listening to Steve talk, I could observe how unassuming and seductive the night was in its descending darkness. It provided a welcome relief from my inner turmoil. I wasn't prepared, though, to let go of my armour just because the weather happened to be nice.

'What are your plans?' Steve asked soon after our conversation began.

'I have no plans', I said defiantly. 'I've worked as an academic, but now I'm an unemployed.' I leaned towards him, a bit too close for such a guarded man, and asked, 'Do you know how it feels? When everything you identify with has been taken away from you?'

He nodded with unexpected understanding.

'What did *you* do?' I asked, intrigued.

'I surrendered', he said with ease.

'You surrendered?'

'When everything seems to fail you, the best thing to do is to try and be at peace with it; look for a purpose rather than fight it. That's the deepest surrender: to be one with what happens to you at every moment.'

When he spoke these words, life seemed to enter his whole being—suddenly and with great power. It was as if a big wave had arrived and swept him away against his own will. The tiredness disappeared from his body and there he was, in front of me, in his own element. At times he got up from his chair and narrated with great vigour, throwing his hands around like dangerous and powerful nets. Then he would sit down again, as if trying to tamp his own intensity down to respectable levels.

And this was the story he told me: In 2000 Steve's marriage had broken down and it looked like he had lost his business as well. He had just enough money to go on a two-week holiday and thought, 'I have these two weeks—what would be the best thing to do?' He had left it open. About a week later, events had started to unfold in his life with repercussions he didn't realise until some time after. First, his friend Alana, a movie director who lived in Los Angeles at the time, had phoned him out of the blue. 'Steve, I think you should come over to Los Angeles and go down to Mexico. Some Mexican Indians have ten-day retreats there: shamanic retreats for discovering and exploring the deeper side of yourself. They act as your guides and take you through it. Mexico is a beautiful country. You would love it. So if you have two weeks free, why don't you come over?'

After that phone conversation Steve had hung up the phone and reflected on the coincidence. This was probably the first time Alana had called him directly from LA. She had somehow connected with him and was inspired to call. Her suggestion sounded enticing. He had always had a longing to go on some kind of mystical or shamanic journey as part of his desire to know more about himself.

About forty-eight hours later he had received another telephone call—again unexpected. Another friend, Savad, was heading off with a small group of researchers to Central Australia to work with some Aboriginal elders who were going to share sacred men's business with a group of whites for the first time. Savad asked, 'There's one place left—would you like it?'

Steve had to think. He had already made up his mind to go to Mexico. 'I'll call you back on this—it's a big decision', he said.

The next day, reason suggested staying in Australia and going on the local journey rather than travelling to Mexico. But he didn't get back to Savad.

Two days later he had received another phone call. This time it was from Alexandra, a friend from Melbourne University. She and her partner were travelling to Sai Baba's ashram in India and invited Steve to come along with them. Steve went home thinking about India. He could easily travel there and stay in their apartment near the ashram.

'It's been a busy week of offers', Steve thought, but he needed some clarity.

He went to see a high school friend, Trevor, at his travel agency in Melbourne. 'If you had two weeks spare, where would you go?'

'Israel!' Trevor exclaimed so spontaneously that something struck a chord with Steve, who jumped out of his seat.

'Yes! Israel!'

Trevor immediately retreated. 'No! I can't send you to Israel! The *Intifada* has just started there! You can't go.'

Steve thought about his inner response when considering Israel. *You don't need to go on a shamanic trip to Mexico to find God.* And as interesting as men's secret rituals in the Australian desert might be, it wasn't what he was looking for. As for the intriguing stories of Sai Baba's miracles in India, he concluded that miracles don't attract people to God. He remembered the story about Jesus feeding the crowds with bread and fish at the lake. Many of those people had come back the next day because they had thought they could get food without working, or because they wanted excitement. They didn't necessarily undergo a spiritual transformation. Steve decided it wasn't that important for him to go to Mexico. It also wasn't essential for him to find out about men's secret business. And he wasn't that interested in finding out about miracles. But the idea of going to Israel was aligned with his life-long interest in *The Urantia Book* and its descriptions of Jesus' life.

Going to Israel, Steve thought, would allow him to connect, in a more personal way, with the teachings of the book and, even more importantly, with its central figure, Jesus. A long time before Steve becoming married or founding a profitable business selling French luxury goods to wealthy Australians, Steve had met Fred Robinson at the Bakehouse, a bakery-cum-alternative shop, on Grenville Street in Melbourne. It was the mid seventies, Steve was in his twenties and looking for 'limitless love and truth', which just happened to be the title of Fred's talk at the Bakehouse. Fred was considered by some of Steve's friends to be a bit of an alternative prophet and Steve decided it was worth his time to meet him. There were only five or six small tables at the Bakehouse, but all were taken by 'seekers of the truth' seated on chairs and tables alike. They were all young, some mighty stoned, and dressed in rainbow-coloured bellbottom pants except Steve, who stood at the back in his jeans and a white T-shirt feeling a little conservative but eager. The intoxicating combination of the smell of fresh baguettes, burning Indian incense and secretly passed joints created a surreal stage for a tall bearded man in his seventies wearing oversized jeans—Fred Robinson. What captivated Steve then was not Fred's status as a New Age patriarch, but his quotes from *The Urantia Book*. After the talk, when the colourful crowd had slowly dispersed, Steve came up to Fred and asked him if he could have a look at the book. Fred passed it to him and Steve browsed through the table of contents. The layout, beginning with the explanation of the nature of the universe and Book IV centring on the life of Jesus, grabbed his attention. Next day he went to the Theosophical Society on Russell Street and bought himself a copy. The book became the spiritual focus of his life. He liked its intellectual consistency. It harmonised heart and mind for him. The next week he quit his office job and drove in his old four-cylinder Wolseley 3500 kilometres from Melbourne to Western Australia to live on Fred's commune. But eventually he decided that he needed to put the book down and return to a normal life. That is, until the year 2000 when the 'normal' seemed to dissolve for him.

Not that he had ever lived a normal life. On the surface, yes. A successful businessman with a taste for fine dining, and a doting father to his daughter. But underneath there was another Steve—the man who spent most of his fortune on supporting unusual projects, such as building accumulators to capture the healing energy of the universe, which in the 1950s Wilhelm Reich named 'orgone'. On her visit to Australia Eva Reich, Wilhelm's daughter, told Steve that if he wanted to continue his 'orgoneic' and spiritual interests, he would have to finance them himself and get into some sort of money-generating business. Importing luxury products from France became that business. So yes, Israel felt like the right thing to do for him. It was like a return to the source for him and a reacquaintance with old passions and interests.

Except the *Intifada*—the second Palestinian uprising—was at its peak at the time. By the time Steve arrived in Israel the millennial Christmas celebrations had been cancelled, and tourists and pilgrims had been advised not to come as the city was considered too dangerous. There was no one around but Steve. The great city of Jerusalem was open to him and he was able to wander around to his heart's content. There were no queues. He saw and studied everything he wished to about Jerusalem, spoke to the people who lived there, and came to understand the culture.

He went to Nazareth next. He wanted to know what Yeshua had been like as a young boy, how difficult life had been for him, what kind of challenges he had faced, how much water he had had to carry and how far the well had been from his home. Simple things.

'And did you?' I asked Steve. 'Did you get to know him better?'

He leaned back in his chair, nodding. 'I did and—whether by stupid chance or design—I made some discoveries in the middle of Jerusalem that would upset any ruling church.'

'You're a heretic!' I said with delight. 'You're a modern heretic.'

'You mean there are more of us?' He asked half-seriously.

'You have no idea!' I laughed. 'Now I need to know what discoveries you made.'

'I can't really tell you . . .'

'What discoveries?' I insisted. 'Mystical? Archaeological? Inner? Outer?'

He nodded. 'All of them: archaeological, mystical. The problem now is I don't know what to do about them and I keep tearing my hair out going back to Jerusalem every year.'

'Why do anything about them?'

'They might have to be protected.'

'Protected from what?'

'I can't tell you', he got up from his chair as if he had said too much already, 'unless I consult Martin about it'.

'Who's Martin?'

'Another traveller.'

The idea of discovery excited me and awoke my curiosity. I felt alive again. I wanted to know what had happened to Steve in Jerusalem. My education in Toronto and studies on religious esoterica at the university there came back to me, together with my old passion for strange heretics and their bizarre ways of finding God. Later on, life would take me in the direction of other, more practical studies, as learning the strange ways of humans searching for God did not guarantee a job at a university. Now I had nothing to lose. I had already lost my job teaching more practical things. And just as well—I could indulge in my old passion.

Steve disappeared into the main house while I stayed behind in the garden. I looked above Richmond at the spring sky, dark and quiet above the noisy street.

'If I have to go through this', I said aloud to the sky, 'through this time of no money and no job, of dealing with my kicking and screaming ambition, then at least make use of me. Make use of me'. I felt an irresistible desire being born in my heart, a desire which had nothing to do with getting back my job and the attendant prestige and money, or appeasing my raging, hurt ambition.

Impulsively, I walked back to the main house, tore a page out of my journal and wrote *I want to go to Jerusalem*. I slipped it under Steve's door and walked away.

As soon as I was back in the studio the panic returned. A terrible, all-encompassing panic mixed with rage, frustration and confusion. I couldn't escape my mind, which was screaming incessantly like a child having a tantrum: *Why is this happening to me? I work hard. I'm smart. I have degrees. I deserve better! I hate being like this!*

My bills were piling up. I went into a stupor of applying for jobs. A mad rush of applications to Melbourne, Sydney, Brisbane, Bendigo, Tasmania, Malaysia, Vietnam, Singapore. When this didn't work I started sending wild applications for jobs that weren't advertised. 'Maybe I need to approach it more from left-field,' I thought, 'since I'm more of a left-fielder anyway'. I sat in meditation and decided I wanted to go to New Mexico or California to teach. I sent a dozen applications there. Each was a gesture of desperation and dread. I responded to unending lists of 'selection criteria' intended to prove you are a total loser because you can't possibly fulfil them all. I became creative. Okay, so they needed something I couldn't do. *Aren't I inventive? Aren't I persuasive? I can convince them I'm the one for the job. You need a lecturer in Communication Studies who can also teach maths in French and is fluent in Mandarin? No problem.* I stayed glued to the computer screen for three days straight, gulping down one coffee after another from my biggest plunger pot. I must have made trips to the kitchen and the toilet, but I couldn't remember them. Had anyone visited me then, they would have found me buried under a pile of discarded papers. The responses to job selection criteria began looking more and more like creative fiction written by a deranged scientist on the verge of a nervous breakdown.

In the midst of this descent into hell, Steve sent me a text message: 'Do you want to come to the Turkish Delight Cafe on Swan Street in Richmond to meet Martin?'

Neither Steve nor Martin was there when I arrived. The cafe was crowded with bohemian, Richmond-style customers dressed in black. The barista at the coffee machine was creating the best coffees in town with the touch of an artist. Each customer was served a latte or a cappuccino with a tiny portrait made of coffee dust on top of the froth. The resemblances were remarkable. I watched him carefully preparing each cup of coffee as I sat at one of the tables. He was quick and composed. His attitude had none of my frantic running and screaming. I glanced at the mirror on the wall by my table. None of the inner tension was visible on my face. This reassured me. I had come prepared after all. In rare moments of sanity, I had researched *The Urantia Book*. As an academic I had more interest in the ancient Gnostic texts; it was as if their age spoke more strongly about their authenticity than a text found in Chicago at the beginning of the twentieth century. Like many religious sources, parts of *The Urantia Book* were apparently channelled during sleep to a neighbour of William and Lena Sadler, well-known Chicago physicians at the time. Their neighbour experienced a restless sleep during which he carried on a theological discourse which he was unaware of upon waking. The Sadlers visited him with a stenographer for over 250 nightly sessions. Apparently this was how parts of the book were transcribed. Other parts, relating more specifically to Jesus' life, had appeared typed on paper in unspecified mysterious circumstances. It is not an unusual story for a Gnostic text: it could be a hoax, could be a revelation. Who was to judge? William Sadler himself had written a book on the delusion of psychic phenomena, and then he met his neighbour . . .

'Joanna?'

I turned, expecting Steve, but instead I saw a man in his sixties resembling an owl. He was of medium build, balding, with glasses hiding highly intelligent eyes that seemed to look inward rather than out at the world. He wore a short-sleeved, striped shirt with navy blue track pants. On his left arm he had a brown linen bag. I took to him immediately.

'I'm Martin. Steve asked me to meet you and tell you about our . . . discovery.' He sat across from me, not showing much interest in my appearance. He was focused and to the point. I liked that.

'Where do you order here?'

I pointed at the barista. 'Coffee?'

'No, a Coke—an old addiction.' Then he added, 'Steve will be here later.'

I nodded.

'Joanna', he began. 'As you know, Steve has been to Israel many times.'

I nodded again.

'He might have told you that after his first trip to Israel he took me there on his subsequent trips and we made some discoveries. We're both readers of the Gnostic Gospels, ancient and modern. So I thought, why not? All the traditional sites were found about three hundred years after Jesus' death. Nobody knows what their sources were. *The Urantia Book* was the most specific so we took some hints from it and began surveying Jerusalem for sites associated with Jesus. Just for fun. And in the middle of Jerusalem, we found a tomb . . .'

'A tomb?'

'Yes. An ancient tomb fitting the description of the tomb where Jesus' body was left.'

I didn't know how to react. My academic, intellectual self wanted to laugh. It wanted to know the details of the methodology of their research. It wanted their research to be based on some ancient sources such as the Dead Sea scrolls, not on a twentieth-century source produced in the sleep of a psychiatrist's neighbour in a Chicago suburb. It wanted their research to be approved by a highly reputable institution backed by big names. The other part of me longed to break free from the restrains of reason and go on a wild adventure, to flow rebelliously with the possibility that their discoveries might be genuine if unorthodox.

'And there's more', he said quietly.

'More?'

'The house where Jesus lived. After that discovery we were left with the dilemma of what to do. Who should we tell about it? And if we did tell somebody, would they destroy the site? Would they believe two Aussie amateurs who'd come to Jerusalem and Nazareth, re-measured the old holy sites and decided they were all in the wrong places. Two Aussie amateurs who claimed they had found the real tomb?'

'I can see your point', I said cautiously.

'We went through the motions of protecting the site. We photographed it, sealed our reports, had them witnessed by a team of lawyers in Melbourne and handed out copies to friends we trusted. Our initial inquiries to the locals regarding the land suggested it belonged to an Islamic *waqf*. A waqf is a sort of trust.' He paused. 'So this is where we are now. We're planning to contact lawyers in Tel Aviv to help us.'

'How did you come around to this . . . project?' I asked, still dazzled but undoubtedly stirred up.

Martin reached for his Coke, opened the can and poured it into the glass. 'I made myself available', he said very seriously. 'I decided to be more proactive with my spiritual growth. I was in my late forties, my kids were grown up, and I stopped working seventy hours a week as an IT programmer. Christmas came and I went to the library and loaded up with books. In one of them I read that my hero, the father of computing Allan Turing, said that the "psychic was real". This gave me quite a shock because until then I believed that psychics, psychic energy were total rubbish! A week later I signed up for a course that looked promising: Psychic training—A practical course. It offered a free information night. Being of Irish-Scottish descent, I'm all for free information. Rob the teacher was an ordained Zen Buddhist monk who had also read *The Urantia Book* and recommended it as a reference book for the course. I was always intrigued with the readings he assigned us. By the time I finished fifteen weeks of his course, I decided the book gave me answers I couldn't find in other sources.'

'What sort of answers?' I asked, intrigued.

Martin looked away for a moment then said, 'Such as a more sober way of looking at Jesus' teachings than my upbringing gave me.'

I could certainly relate to this. No matter how hard I tried to be a good Catholic, the stories I had been given sounded at best like fairy tales. Yet I was not convinced that *The Urantia Book* was much better in this respect.

'But', I began tentatively, 'there are some parts of the book that are a bit strange . . .'

'That never bothered me. In my profession I had to deal with masses of material and select what was useful and move quickly past what wasn't. The book made the whole story of Jesus real for me—that's why I thought the locations of his life and death could be real as well. So when I met Steve at a barbeque at a mutual friend's home, we were already more or less kindred spirits and developed a friendship immediately. He told me about his first trip to Israel. He had a real need to share what had happened there. He showed a brief report of his trip with photographs of the house in Nazareth he thought could have been Yeshua's house, and I thought it was the most amazing thing. Imagine if this is really the house? So when he offered to take me to Israel, in the role of a computer programmer,' he winked at me, 'I made a list of things for and against the trip.' He then leaned toward the small linen bag that he brought with him and carefully took out a piece of yellowish paper. 'This is the list!' He put it down on the table between us. 'As you can see, I couldn't find anything against it. On the "for" side of the list, I wrote . . .' he took off his glasses, picked up the list again and held it a fair distance from his eyes the way long-sighted people do and read aloud to me, 'number one, I am fascinated by Steve's story; number two, Steve would be a good tour guide'. He interrupted himself for a moment and added, 'I was correct. Steve is a good tour guide'.

Martin continued, 'Number three, I would tour the Holy Land, which I had been taught so much about by the Church; and number four, Steve was a trusted friend and I wanted to share his experiences with him'. He put the list down and with the same care he took it out put it back into his linen bag. 'These are the external reasons for joining Steve', he said as he put his glasses back on after giving them a closer look and cleaning them with the serviette from the table.

'And any other reasons?' I picked up on his theme.

He took out a two-dollar coin from his wallet, held it between two fingers and said, 'Look at this coin. The coin parable is my favourite. The coin has lost its shine because it's covered in mundane dust. The dust is your job, your career, what your parents told you, what is expected of you at work and at home. But underneath it all is the great shiny truth, the unimaginable possibility of a much richer, more fulfilling life. Have you ever thought about how it might feel to follow an inner intelligence that goes against our socialised knowledge of how things should be? Nothing would change externally—you would still do everything you used to do—but your whole world would be transformed internally. This is what the trip to Jerusalem did to me'.

I listened intently. 'That makes me think I should drop everything and join an ashram or a monastery somewhere, and get out of the rat race once and for all.' I laughed self-consciously. 'This is my recurring fantasy.'

Martin didn't look at me. Sitting straight, he seemed to be watching the busy tables in the cafe. It was a trendy place, with its round tables and their beautiful metalwork I used to take for granted in Europe but had now learned to appreciate fully. The food counter was overflowing with Middle Eastern delicacies arranged on colourful ceramic plates: hummus, *baba ghanoush*, eggplants, roasted carrots and capsicum. Then there were the sweets: little pastries filled with nuts, soaking in honey. A couple walked in and took a table in front of us. Both were dressed in black. The woman especially looked very stylish, in a grungy, almost carefree, way that was also perfectly arranged— from her hair to her designer shoes. They had two small children with them, perhaps three and five years of age, who insisted on *babycinos* the moment they climbed into their chairs. Despite its strange combination of bohemian and yuppie elements, the place retained the sensual appeal of the Middle East.

Martin turned to me again and said, 'You don't have to move into a monastery to live a spiritual life. But sometimes some isolation from the mundane is necessary so we can bring back the shine to the coin'.

How do you bring shine back to the coin? I asked myself while stirring my latte, disturbing the barista's coffee-ground portrait of me. We are covered by the dust of our habitual living. And while we do lots of worthwhile things, such as raising a family or having a career, we are not conscious of the inner potential beneath our daily routines. We don't ask ourselves the most important questions: Where am I in all of these things? Where am I hiding in all of these personas?

'Here he is', I heard Martin say. I saw Steve heading in our direction, his head towering above Martin and me for a moment until he sat down.

'Did you have a chance to catch up?' he asked.

'I told Joanna about our mad idea to protect the tomb'.

'Did she like it?' Steve turned to me with his question.

I smiled. 'Strangely enough, I did'.

'These are pictures of the tomb'. Steve took out some pictures from his briefcase.

19

There was not much to see: a cave-like opening in the middle of an area looking like a garbage pit. I told them what I thought.

'It's an unauthorised garbage pit, right in the middle of the city. The land looks abandoned, which is strange as it must be a very valuable piece of property for developers.' Steve looked at me in his probing way again.

'Until two guys from Australia come along and claim this to be Jesus' tomb?' I asked jokingly.

'Something like that. Is it hard to believe?' He asked the question as if wanting to test me.

'No, not necessarily', I said sincerely. 'I like the idea of impossible things.'

'That's interesting', Steve paused. 'Did you say you were a medieval scholar?'

'I used to be, but I strayed. I began studying more practical things that I thought would earn me a better living, but my love is still there. For the Gnostics. And the heretics. And the mad pilgrims and mystics looking for signs of a divine presence in our lives.' I laughed. 'There are too many things to learn about—human and divine.'

I was surprised at speaking to them so spontaneously. In my professional life, the loss of which I had grieved so recently, I wouldn't have dared express these things for fear of being seen as a flake.

Steve listened carefully to my words while Martin seemed completely lost in the pleasure of his Coke.

'Martin and I and some other associates decided to form a private trust to buy the land in Jerusalem.'

'To buy the land?' I asked with disbelief. 'Wouldn't it be extremely expensive?'

'There is money for it', Steve said with quiet assurance. He talked about money as a natural and plentiful occurrence in life. I wished I could feel the same.

'To do what? Excavations?'

'Probably. But mostly to protect the land, to preserve it for future generations.'

'As a holy site?'

'Yes.'

I felt suspicious of any religious fundamentalism, so I asked, 'Just for Christians?'

'No . . . for all religions, for all people. Call it a place of peace in Jerusalem—*The Peace Garden*. How does that sound? We're here to find ourselves and to do good, right?'

I liked the idea. I liked these two men.

Then Steve surprised me even more. 'In what role, what capacity, would you like to come with us to Jerusalem?'

I stiffened with expectation. 'I'd like to come along as a chronicler of your adventure. You know, I don't think it's important that what you've discovered is the tomb. But I'm interested in the journey it has started.'

They both looked at me as if wanting to check my sincerity.

'What sort of chronicle would it be?' Martin asked.

'A book', I responded with unexpected certainty.

Walking back to the studio in Steve's garden I considered the extraordinary thing that had just happened. From a 'normal' point of view the whole story was mad. Yet from another point of view it made perfect sense. I'd never wanted the small stabilisations: the house in the suburbs and a good pension plan. All my life I had been trying to escape the parametres of 'normal' life (to settle down, make money, have a family and a mortgage), which were too narrow for me. When I was a young woman I was quite dismissive of that paradigm. It signified a lacking to me. There was no choice-making in it. You just followed what everybody else around you had always done. There was no growth in it. I was looking for intensity of experience, for passion in life, for glimpses of the miraculous behind the ordinary. I'd travelled around the world to exotic places, taken in magnificent views and drunk wisdom from different cultures to quench my thirst and strip myself of those prescriptive layers designed by other people, systems, churches, governments. When I finished my Ph.D I convinced myself it was time to settle for a career and a house. But every time I decided to settle it was because somehow, somewhere in the process of accomplishing things, I had lost touch with my soul.

In my letterbox I found three more rejections to my job applications. I felt sick when I thought of my future. For the first time in my life I saw no future for myself—none of my careful plans had worked. Except now I sat down on the couch, thinking that perhaps when everything we identify with is burned to the ground we can then rebuild ourselves in a more meaningful way. As painful as it was thinking about it, there was the slight possibility a marvellous gift was hidden under the disguise of my confusion and turmoil. A gift of realisation that I was not *that* turmoil. I was not *that* ambition. And if I was not them, who was I? I got off the couch and threw the three rejection letters in the bin.

WALKING IN HOLY MADNESS

Before I left for Jerusalem, people kept telling me that the Holy Land is a mad place riven by hatred. But it is passion for God that drives people insane there. Anyone who sees the city only as a centre of political struggle completely misses the point. I don't believe anyone who has ever entered Jerusalem can think of it other than as a city of immense energy which is both necessary for, and corrupting of, love. Jerusalem turns out to be the most powerful place I have ever visited. In Jerusalem every site is a symbol imprinted on your consciousness, asking you to face all your demons. A place where people have travelled and made pilgrimages for nearly four thousand years.

In western culture the idea of travel as pilgrimage is at least as old as the Middle Ages. And this concept was, quite possibly, invented to enable people to find some freedom and a taste for adventure. Sometimes pilgrimages can take on a more profound turn than originally intended and we can discover as much of our inner landscape as we do of the external. Travel and pilgrimage are about getting away from normality, giving space to your Self, opening up to whatever revelations might happen. Sometimes the pilgrimage manifests as a spontaneous need to experience the new, the unknown that is hidden in us—that which demands to be revealed and experienced away from known, familiar circles. At first glance such a need might appear to be irrational, even irresponsible, but it is also somehow necessary, exciting and irresistibly compelling.

Our case is no different. We arrive in the early morning hours in Amman, Jordan's capital, but our connecting flight is delayed for a few hours. Martin negotiates with the airlines for a room and meal for us at the airport hotel. We agree to share one room to maintain camaraderie—it feels good to be together. To share a space before the great adventure. We do our best to cover our nervousness in small tasks. We shower in turns and go downstairs to check out the hotel. The lobby is busy with a few hundred Muslim pilgrims from Sri Lanka, both women and men dressed in impeccable white. I observe my companions. Steve seems to be gliding, powered by some invisible energy. His movements are both premeditated and flamboyant, even when he takes our pictures in the lobby. Martin is unusually agitated for a computer geek. He trips over the steps on his way to the dining room, runs to the buffet, then can't decide which table we should sit at. We have a meal: Middle Eastern flatbread with salad. I can't eat much. My stomach is churning with the expectation of Jerusalem and what awaits us there. I know that both Martin and Steve's minds are already there, guessing the state of the tomb or whether someone has already got hold of their discovery. Eventually we grab a taxi back to the airport and board a tiny, shaky Airbus for Tel Aviv that does its best not to fall out of the sky. At Tel Aviv airport we learn our luggage has been left behind in Bangkok.

'What's your religion?' a young female airport guard asks me, the first sign of how religion dominates human interactions in the Holy Land. She reminds me of an overeager girl scout, but, unlike other girl scouts, she carries a big gun. Her petite frame seems to drown within the oversized khaki uniform of the Israeli army and her young dimpled face is stern and reproaching.

'Well, I was born a Catholic, but now I'm . . . experimenting', I reply.

'Experimenting with what?'

'I practise meditation and . . . er . . . read about mystical religious traditions.'

'Eh?'

'Esoteric Tantric teachings, Sufi poets, Rumi, Gnostic Gospels . . .'

The line between her eyebrows deepens. 'What . . . gospels?'

'Jesus' teachings which were hidden by the Church.'

She lets out a professional sigh as if to say, 'Another bunch of Christian lunatics looking for salvation!' and yells right in my face, 'Full security check!'

The young man from security is a Mediterranean cherub of surprising beauty with wisps of curly dark hair falling over his face. I am immediately inclined to be more forgiving of his behaviour, even if he chooses to be rude. But he asks softly, in a slightly confused tone, 'Are you looking for some . . . mystics?'

I catch myself assessing my own sanity. How many crazy people of all faiths come to Jerusalem? I feel suddenly exhausted. 'I'm looking for myself', I say with unexpected honesty.

He looks at me with a smile and lets me go without asking any more questions.

It is the Sabbath and there are no public buses to Jerusalem from the airport. A private taxi driver approaches Steve and tries to negotiate a price for a ride to Jerusalem.

'No', I hear Steve. 'That's twice as much as I paid last time.'

'You'll get nowhere without me! Nowhere!' the taxi driver yells behind our backs.

'I think he's confusing us with his ex-wife', I laugh off his fiery temperament. When you are told something can't happen, look for another door to open. Five minutes later a minibus pulls over in front of us. The driver leans out the window and asks, 'Jerusalem?'

From the window of the minibus I gaze at the strange, arid landscape and the naked buildings, with their unfamiliar pale colours. The buildings look like part of a public housing establishment. On balconies with old pink and yellowish paint abandoned pieces of furniture are stored and left in the open: a fridge leaning diagonally over the whole length of the balcony and a coffee table with a missing leg. Three dark-haired children play in front of the building and wave at us, somewhat cautiously, as the minibus passes. The whole place has the sense of a refugee camp. The road becomes more curved as the minibus struggles round the corners. Suddenly the buildings change. They are now elegant, with small French balconies and potted flowers on display. The streets are filled with well-dressed people rushing through the city. As we approach the American Colony Hotel, the city changes again. It is like entering a different place, ancient and heavy with history. The streets become narrower and occasionally we see Palestinian men standing in small groups, smoking cigarettes.

The driver drops us off in front of the American Colony Hotel. He doesn't want to go any deeper into the Palestinian section where our hotel, the Seven Arches, is. I breathe in the air of the city.

'Is this the Old City?' I ask in expectation. 'Is this where the tomb is?' My heart is pounding, as if I am waiting to meet an old lover with whom I have an unfinished history.

'No, but it's very close', Martin says to me, then he turns to Steve and says, 'I'll walk to the tomb and check if it's been touched or uncovered.'

Steve, suddenly serious, nods. 'Be careful.'

'What about us? Can't we see it now?' I whinge to Steve as I watch Martin walking off.

'Not now. If everything is in order, you'll see it soon enough. We don't want to draw unnecessary attention to the site. It might look suspicious: three foreigners hovering over the same place over and over again.' I follow Steve to reception where he organises a taxi to our hotel. The young woman at reception offers us a hot chocolate while we wait. I am cold and tired. When we were leaving Melbourne I wasn't sure what sort of weather we could expect in Jerusalem; I'd read that Jerusalem was much colder than Tel Aviv. They were right: the December wind cuts through my bones. The American Colony Hotel is like a luxurious Bedouin tent dressed up for the arrival of important guests. To the left side of the reception hangs a plaque bearing the names of distinguished guests who have visited the hotel. Lawrence of Arabia is among them. I touch the plaque as material proof that I am finally here. Steve sits on the arm chair, his back stiff with expectation.

In about fifteen minutes, Martin is back. His Akubra hat is falling diagonally across his face and makes him look like a dishevelled messenger. He exclaims in a loud voice, turning heads at the lobby, 'It's there! It's there and I think it's untouched!'

Steve gets up with visible relief on his face as the receptionists tells us our taxi is waiting.

'Oh my God! So it's still here, untouched', I mumble in excitement to Steve. 'What now?'

'First, we go to our hotel', he orders. 'And then we rest.'

We collapse into the taxi. 'It's there and it's untouched', reverberates in our jetlagged minds.

Outside, the reality of the division of the city into different religious parts begins to dawn on me. The Jewish drivers only take you so far, then there is a quick switch to Palestinian drivers, depending on where you are in the city. No transgressions to these rules are welcome. As evening approaches it begins to turn dark, but I manage to catch a view of an older Palestinian man walking his camel up the steep hill. Our hotel is just on the outskirts of old Jerusalem, at the top of the Mount of Olives. By the time we arrive at the Seven Arches Hotel I am so exhausted I feel like one of the walking dead. I wave 'see you' to Steve, who walks into the room next to mine, then wave to Martin as he is heading into the room across the hall. I fall onto my bed fully dressed.

After some time I wake up and, still full of sleep, remember my first dream in Jerusalem. *I am walking along one of the city's streets looking for something lost when I notice a young man lying on the sidewalk. Someone whom I can only vaguely see is trying to help the young man. I think, 'It's nice of this person to try to help the man lying on the sidewalk, but it's hopeless'. I am convinced the man is beyond help. He lies there covered by repulsive mucous; his face is horribly deformed, swollen and covered with blood and spit. He is two-dimensional, completely flat, an annoying remnant of some forgotten suffering. There is no point helping this disfigured creature. Despite the initial impulse to run to his aid, I pass him by, intensely sickened by the grotesque vision of his suffering.*

I am frustrated with myself. How can an intelligent, educated person like me have such a dream? I sit on my bed and look through the window at the glorious view of the Old City:

the Golden Dome right in front. The holiest site for both Jew and Muslim. The city, known for its power to infect otherwise perfectly rational people with 'Jerusalem fever', has already cast its spell on me. Regular, sceptical citizens of the world come here and become preachers, discover they are messiahs, are overcome by other religious psychoses. After a while I understand that the dream makes perfect sense. It has brought back to the surface subconscious images of Jesus created by our society and religious institutions in particular: the suffering, the unimaginable and grotesque—things I can't relate to. Even as a child these were concepts I couldn't connect with, despite my Catholic upbringing. How could a child really comprehend something as terrifying as images of a suffering Christ—a skeletal, tragic figure with blood dribbling from his hands and feet, as if painted by some morbid masochists? As a little girl I stood in church in front of these paintings, horrified and puzzled at the same time. Horrified by the suffering. Puzzled by the convoluted explanations for this suffering—explanations which were always based around the notions of people as 'bad' or 'sinners'.

I pour myself a glass of water from the jar on the night table and think about all the synods and theological disputes on the comparative amounts of the divine and human natures in Jesus. They all seem superficial to me in the face of the natural human desire to know another human being—human or divine—intimately through his or her struggles. I remember as a medieval studies student learning about the early church synods when the dogma was formulated, when the possibility of interpretation was closed, when the chance for a personal relationship with Jesus was almost completely denied. Powerful bishops, theologians and emperors were involved in deciding the degree of humanity or divinity within Jesus. *The degree?*

As if the greatness of a being of that spiritual calibre could be measured. Some believed he was an eternal being incarnated in Mary's womb. They stressed Jesus' divinity. This posed a problem, because if he were fully divine and without a human element then his suffering on the cross becomes problematic.

Did he really suffer? Can God suffer? If not, the whole story of his suffering for humankind is difficult to substantiate. Others, notably Paul, Bishop of Antioch around 260 AD, insisted that Jesus was fully human and became God at the moment of his baptism by John the Baptist. Was there some kind of enlightenment, a sudden realisation of his Godhood through grace? I didn't have a problem with that. This would mean he was, like us, human, and became realised through spiritual practice, like many other great beings. This, however, would make him *a* god and not *the* God, and some people would definitely have difficulty accepting that. I wasn't that concerned at what point in his life he had become the great spirit, the Christ consciousness, at one with the One. I wanted mainly to relate to him as I would to another human being. A great being who was misunderstood by people who professed faith in him.

Steve knocks on my door so I put on the jeans and blouse I wore on the airplane (I am still waiting for my luggage).

'The tomb?' I ask, expecting he will take me there now.

'No, not today', he smiles at my impatient anticipation. 'Today you'll see the Old Jerusalem, the city where Yeshua spent his last hours. Nothing in his story makes sense unless you *feel* Jerusalem first.'

'Really?' I tease him.

Steve laughs jovially, 'Jerusalem makes people mad with passion for God. In this city you can feel the great energy—an energy so huge it makes people do unspeakable things.'

'Like looking for Yeshua's tomb?' I mock him gently. Steve is not worried. 'Aha! So watch out!' I allow him to take charge today and I am eager to surrender to the city. We walk down the hall to Martin's room. Martin too is already being carried along by the energy of the place, completely caught up in the swirling pool of excitement the city somehow creates. There is a certain power—a mad, sublime power—in this city which has no explanation. We find Martin in his room with the door wide open. He is rushing around the room in a strange frenzy with nothing on but his underwear and a half-wet t-shirt he has washed the previous night. Martin, the solid, stable computer programmer and family man.

'I can't believe', I say to Martin, 'that some people, out of fear, won't visit the Old City. Why travel all the way to Jerusalem and not see it?' For me, Jerusalem *is* the Old City and the small area around it, including the American Colony Hotel.

And so we set out for Old Jerusalem.

We walk to the Palestinian quarter of the Old City, to the Holy Sepulchre. On the Palestinian side of the Old City the world is a *souk*—a great market extending endlessly through long and narrow medieval streets. A fragrant world of exotic spices: cinnamon, cardamom, tumeric, cumin seeds and ground cumin, sesame seeds, *za'tar* made from thyme, and *sumac*, fiery ground paprika. It is easy to imagine the medieval world here again, the merchants smelling the cardamom and appreciating the local delicacies, sumac and za'tar. Old women still sit on cobbled streets the way they have sat for centuries selling greens, parsley, spinach, garlic, spices and anything saleable. The women, dressed in black, are sometimes toothless and without smiles, but with the familiar contentment of those who have accepted their life as it is. All the people who have passed by the buildings: the rabbis, the monks, the Muslims going to the mosque, the Crusaders in their mad passion for the Holy Land and the riches hidden there. The city's complicated history pulses on the streets and is strangely elating.

The area around the Holy Sepulchre is crowded with souvenir and *devotionalia* shops selling all manner of Jesus-related kitsch. Among them Steve manages to find stores with expensive Persian carpets. These stores, which appear like crevices in the narrow streets, have second and third floors with elaborate staircases. The kitsch is up the front; the beautiful carpets and antiques are hidden on upper floors. Martin and I accompany Steve for a while in his search for a carpet with a Tree of Life design: the type of Persian carpet with a tree in the middle and many floral elements and birds sitting on its branches. Martin explains that after conversations with their friend and explorer Robert Sarmast, Steve has become convinced some of the ancient designs show scenes from the Garden of Eden, which Robert believes is the sunken part of the Eastern Mediterranean—hence Robert's lifelong obsession with Atlantis.

While Steve looks at different carpets, Martin carefully bends to lace his runners tighter, then slowly picks himself up, his hands holding his back as if trying to conceal a pain. 'Feeling my age, Joanna', he says in a dry, matter-of-fact way. From the little brown linen bag that hangs on his shoulder he takes out sunscreen and carefully places small bits of the cream on his temples. I watch how precise his every move is.

'I think I should explain to you that Robert is the reason for Steve's travels to Cyprus. Robert is an Iranian American—and is harassed by everyone because of it. He has to be careful when going to Iran because he is American. He can't go to Israel because he is an Iranian. This sort of nonsense, you know.' Martin adjusts his hat and stirs us towards the shady part of the street. 'Two years ago, we learned about him at the Urantia Conference. We read his book about Atlantis and when we were in Jerusalem we went to Cyprus where Robert was based at the time and met him. At that time Steve was thinking about helping Robert raise funds for his project. You see, Robert had identified the sea around Cyprus as Atlantis. He speculated that the story of Atlantis and the story of the Garden of Eden were one and the same. His main source was Plato, who wrote in a serious manner about Atlantis in *The Republic*. So far Robert has been unable to prove his theory. He's been ridden with technological problems, as he couldn't physically reach under the sea-floor. On a previous expedition he thought he had found man-made walls and a canal, but just before they got to the crucial point they had a computer meltdown. Now he is touring the US raising funds for a new expedition.'

I think of the two men I am travelling with and about Robert. We are like children searching for our mothers. *Where did we come from? What are our beginnings?* No one in our company of seekers doubts Darwin, but the theory of evolution ignores one essential aspect of the human psyche—the soul and the striving for the divine. Robert, Steve and Martin have been searching for this in a committed, passionate way. They have been aware of how their search looks to others—one eccentric expedition after another. But what is there to lose? Even the smallest insight into our souls is a fair prize for me. I have always preferred the idea of uncovering hidden knowledge—knowledge some individuals throughout the ages continuously hide for their own reasons. Uncovering this knowledge is like practising archaeology of the psyche. It requires us to bypass logic at times and witness whatever our common subconscious mind might throw at us. A secret design on an ancient carpet, a hidden tomb, a submerged continent—aren't these the soul itself?

I look around for Steve. In his jeans and impeccable white T-shirt he stands in the front of the shop with Persian carpets and has an esoteric exchange with a shopkeeper about the Garden of Eden. He is completely at ease in this environment. The shopkeeper too forgets the business of selling for a moment and indulges himself in conversation with the foreigner on matters of creation and its representation on the carpets.

'It's an ancient and secret knowledge accessible only to the initiated', I hear the shopkeeper saying as Steve points to a design on one of the carpets.

I nudge Martin to go and enter the Holy Sepulchre. Construction of it began in the fourth century. In 325 CE Emperor Constantine agreed to build a basilica on the site of an ancient Roman temple in Jerusalem. His mother, Empress Helena, was trekking around the Holy Land trying to find places associated with Yeshua. This wasn't an easy task: after the Jewish rebellion in 70 CE, the Romans destroyed many buildings and the local Christian community was very small and divided. Jerusalem was the centre of Jewish Christianity; that is, the faith of those Jews who followed Yeshua's teachings but saw them as fully embedded in other Judaic teachings or supplemental to them. In many respects they were strictly Orthodox, and Yeshua's teachings were an extension of what they already practised. The first bishop of Jerusalem was

Yeshua's brother Ya'akov (in Aramaic, or James in the Latinised version of the name). He had joined his brother's movement quite late. I suppose as a brother he had needed some extra convincing: 'What . . . my brother . . . the Son of God?'

Ya'akov worked hard to reconcile the Jewish followers of Yeshua in Jerusalem, with Yeshua's Gentile followers recruited from all over the Mediterranean by Paul. Paul, the ex-tax collector, preached the uniqueness of Yeshua's teaching and was convinced one didn't need to be Jewish to be Christian. Which sounds like an oxymoron after two thousand years of anti-Semitism and mutual antagonism between what later became two faiths. At its inception, Christianity, as far as Ya'akov and his congregation were concerned, was just another branch of Judaism. The Christianity that developed through the Middle Ages as a completely separate religion from Judaism was more or less created by Paul. Paul wanted Yeshua's teaching to be accessible to everyone—Jewish or not. How his intention to spread Yeshua's teachings to the Gentiles turned into two-thousand-years-and-counting of antagonism and hatred is a paradox. In April 2002 an urn of Ya'akov was found. An Israeli collector showed the urn to Professor Andre Lemaire of the Sorbonne. To Lemaire's surprise the inscription on the urn was in Aramaic, Yeshua's first language. The inscription stated: 'Ya'akov, son of Yosef, brother of Yeshua'. Historical evidence on Yeshua's brother became more widely available when the amazing story of this discovery was described in *The Brother of Jesus*, a book by Hershel Shanks (an editor of *Biblical Archaeology Review*) and Ben Witherington III (a biblical scholar).

The building of the Holy Sepulchre was primarily a political act. The new Emperor Constantine converted to Christianity and ordered many churches built: a church in Jerusalem made perfect sense. Constantine was also a diplomat and didn't want to destroy the existing pagan Roman temple on the site unless there was convincing evidence it had been the place where Yeshua's body was put to rest. As the story goes, Bishop Macarius was eager to find that evidence. Whether their intentions were sincere and he believed it was a place of Yeshua's burial, or whether he just wanted to destroy the pagan temple and build a Christian basilica on its ruins is anyone's guess. Archaeologists and historians around the world still argue about this. I don't particularly respect Christian bishops from that time. For example, St Cyril, Bishop of Alexandria, ordered the first female librarian (and a philosopher) from the famous Alexandrian library killed by a mob because she wasn't a Christian. Why the Catholic Church made him into a Saint has always been beyond me.

As for Macarius, all we know is that he didn't have evidence from the start, but he was determined to build a Christian basilica on the Roman site. He had lobbied for the basilica before anything was found under the pagan temple. Macarius was a good example of determination. *Seek and ye shall find.* He found a first-century Jewish tomb under the temple and pronounced that it was the tomb of Yeshua. It might well have been. The Emperor gave permission to destroy the pagan temple and so the Holy Sepulchre was built. Even today it is divided into several sections, each one of them belonging to a different Christian denomination which existed in the Middle Ages.

Inside, Martin and I join a long queue of pilgrims waiting to see the tomb, the *Edicule*, which is now under the shared care of the Eastern Orthodox, Roman Catholic and Armenian Apostolic Churches. It is not a very private experience.

The tomb is in a small cave-like enclosure. An Armenian monk at the entrance allows between two to four people at a time to enter the small two-roomed space. Some behave in a devotional way and pray; others behave like curious but generally disinterested tourists. Perhaps they are agnostics looking on it as a cultural artefact. I don't know. I pray there, but I don't have any spiritual experience. Once I reach the tomb I see two young European men hesitantly cross themselves above it, as if the automatic gesture is something they have inherited from their childhoods. They have an interest in the place and questions in their minds. They too are looking for something here, but aren't sure if they have found it or responded to it appropriately.

Then again, what is an 'appropriate' response to a place like this? Neither Steve nor Martin believes that the Holy Sepulchre is the place of crucifixion or the real tomb, but many do. What should we feel here, apart from reverence? A reverence for all the people who have come here believing, trusting, hoping this is the tomb of Jesus, a sign of the divine and miraculous in their lives.

I wander away to a smaller basilica on a lower level. The place is a medieval labyrinth: a dark space with unexpected nooks, winding stairways that can take you to yet another dark corridor as if to conceal a secret treasure. I would have loved it as a child—a perfect place for the ultimate mystery. The place appears to be empty. I sit on a small wooden bench against the wall and the strange, powerful spirit of the city overwhelms me again. I hear the cries and voices of Crusaders trying to explain themselves to me, trying to tell me about their zeal and cruelty, their devotion, about their sins and suffering, asking me to understand them. I am relieved when Steve finds me and I snap out of this medieval time warp of sensations.

We have lunch in the Jewish Old City, a very different place from the Palestinian Old City, with its medieval markets and fragrant spices. We are suddenly walking in a very organised city, with clearly marked streets, expensive-looking souvenir shops with Jewish religious symbols in silver and maps of Jewish archaeological sites in Jerusalem, and cafes with Israeli hummus and European cappuccinos. Young soldiers, both men and women, walk around with their guns. On guard. Anything can happen anytime here, their presence says. Usually Orthodox Jews are the people who choose to live in the Old City. The liberal and modernised Israeli prefers the newer parts of Jerusalem or even Tel Aviv. Anywhere but Jerusalem—to avoid the political problems and religious drama. This polarity makes people aware of what is going on around them, it asks people to make moral choices and take political stands. More and more I have come to believe that in many cases the situation is far too complex to take a clear stand on a particular side. Taking a strong political or religious stand always demands that we make judgments about others and their beliefs, and it inevitably sets us apart from others, regardless of how worthy and just the cause.

In the Jewish part of Old Jerusalem it is difficult to form the same impression. Underneath their defiance, people here are sad too. They sit in cafes, watch school children play in the sun and at the same time wait for a bomb to strike them. The possibility of attack shows in their nervousness as they look around, joke with the young soldiers as if seeking their reassurance, discuss any recent attacks in the area. I remember from my own experience of martial law in Poland how the presence of soldiers on the streets affected us. Once I was returning home from visiting a friend and I saw a group of armed soldiers walking in my direction. My heart stopped in panic. I did not have my ID on me, which in itself was a crime. I felt my whole body sweating in fear as they passed by me. In Jewish Old Jerusalem the soldiers are always present, always expecting the worst—expecting to be brutally expelled from the city they love and claim only for themselves. I wonder how any one group can claim such an ancient city, whether Jewish or Muslim or Christian. How could you claim what history has complicated throughout the ages? The city is too old, too magnificent, too otherworldly for *anyone* to claim. There is no sign of any peaceful resolution in the Old City, neither from the Jewish nor the Palestinian sides. I doubt that anyone could claim more than a five-minute stretch of the city.

I walk along with Steve and Martin thinking about this, thinking also about how different Old Jerusalem is from, say, Caulfield in Melbourne, where the Jewish Orthodox population lives comfortably. Caulfield is a green, affluent and peaceful migrant suburb. There is no defiance there. The Jewish part of Old Jerusalem is an attempt, after two-thousand years, to reclaim a lost home—an attempt suffused with the sadness of knowing such reclamation is futile.

After lunch we proceed to the Wailing Wall. Steve and Martin wait for me as I go by myself over to the women's side. A friend from Melbourne instructed me to say a prayer for her father and leave a note in the wall with her father's name, Zvi. Many other women are doing the same thing: praying and leaving small pieces of paper in the wall. On both sides, male and female, white notes climb the wall with requests to God. I have always wondered about this. About all our requests to God. Does He—if God is somehow gendered—have a filing cabinet? If He/She/It does, the cabinet must be infinite. This is a part of the human condition—to need this connection, to seek this kind of Friend. Didn't the Sufis call God 'the Friend', or even 'the Lover'?

I like this part of Hindu teaching the most. The Omniscient Friend is a legitimate part of us, something present in us—only we are seldom aware of this, lost in our games of desire and repulsion. *I want that. I don't want that.* If we could only sit for a moment and reflect deeply on the world and ourselves, we would find the Friend within. The Friend, the Self, God. The difficulty is in getting to that part of us and being able to stay in touch with it. Would this make us all-powerful? Probably not, but it would make us content. It would end the sense of emptiness, the sense that there must be something, someone, more. The initial dissatisfaction that sets us on our search.

My Catholic upbringing has created lots of 'divine' confusion in me. The bizarre combination of the all-loving-yet-punishing Father and His Son—who for not entirely clear reasons died in an awful way. The idea of redemption through Jesus has never been fully comprehensible to me. This idea assumes the original sinfulness of human beings, which I can't agree with. A sinfulness so bad it had to be redeemed by the Son of God. Too abstract for me. Is it easier for the Jewish people by the Wall with their one God who has chosen them? Even here I have a problem: why would God, the Divine All-Embracing-Consciousness, the Friend, have a preference for some races over others?

Like other women, I walk away from The Wall without turning my back to it. The Wall itself is a powerful symbol of the city and its 'holy fever'. The Temple, the Mosque, and the Golden Dome on Mount Moriah. How can one argue with places like this? For both faiths Mount Moriah is *the* place of Creation. The navel of the world. The Jews call it *Shetiyah*, or 'drinking', as it is the fountain of primeval waters from which the world is created. The Muslims believe it to be the abyss where the 'well of souls' is located. The rock is supposed to be made of stones from the Garden of Eden. This is the place where Abraham brought his only son to sacrifice to God. This is where Solomon built the First Temple. The Temple was expanded during Yeshua's times; he taught here and impressed the scholarly rabbis with his wisdom. But the Romans destroyed the Temple after the Jewish uprising of 70 CE and after the Temple's destruction, the site became covered with rubbish. Six hundred years later, Caliph Omar cleared the rubbish and constructed the first wooden mosque. Another four hundred years later the Crusaders killed everybody and named the place the Temple of Solomon. A hundred years after that the Moslems reclaimed the city, the Crusaders left, and the mosque was rebuilt. The mosque is now situated where the Temple of Solomon had once been. The Zionists built a ramp so they could climb to the mosque, take over the site and rebuild the Temple of Solomon in its place. Soldiers with guns guard the ramp. On 28 September 2000, just before Steve's first visit to Jerusalem, Ariel Sharon, Israeli opposition leader at the time, defiantly entered the mosque and stood there renewing the claim. On the same day, riots broke out and faithful on both sides were killed. That same year Bill Clinton tried to restore peace in Jerusalem.

The threatening, elevating power of the place is overwhelming. Human fervour, normally directed at other human beings, is directed in Jerusalem towards the ownership of God. Ownership in any relationship is always problematic. What about ownership of God? That all-consuming ardour is magnified infinitely when directed at God and His temples. When you are in Jerusalem you feel the POWER. Only in a place like Jerusalem does the Almighty seem to come to mind naturally. In a city like this, you just long for someone to run naked through Jerusalem—like John Safran, a young iconoclast filmmaker from Melbourne did—with nothing on but a beanie and a scarf.

We stop at Ali Baba Cafe near Via Dolorosa, where, as tradition says, Yeshua carried the cross through Jerusalem on the day of his crucifixion. We sit down and are ordering coffees and small pastries filled with honey and pistachios when we see a group of zealous Christians carrying a wooden cross. I stare at them in amazement.

The young Palestinian owner of the cafe says, 'They're moving from the Fourth to the Fifth Station of the Cross, here . . . around the corner'. He points with his finger. 'This is where the Christians believe the Fifth Station is, where Simon of Cyrene helped Jesus carry the cross.'

'How do you know that?' Steve asks.

'Christian tourists make my business', the young man responds in a matter-of-fact way.

I observe the people eager to relive Yeshua's torment. Whatever their intention, it creates a bizarre effect for onlookers. Western men and women, dressed in jeans, t-shirts and Nike shoes are carrying a wooden cross through the narrow streets of the city of Jerusalem. 'No wonder Jews and Muslims think we're a bit nutty', I catch myself thinking. Look at that! If I have a problem with suffering being a part of life and the focus on Yeshua's suffering in particular rather than on his teachings, these people have steeped themselves in it with great fervour.

What does this have to do with his teachings? I want to start a tirade but stop, remembering I am in the city of Holy Madness where no act of religious allegiance, however eccentric, is considered strange. I look at my companions. Martin ignores the whole scene, busily looking through his labyrinthine set of notes. It is a sort of organised chaos of loose papers filled in with tiny but immaculately shaped streams of words. Each miniscule but flawless word legible only to him. As he reads through the notes, he underlies some of them with his fountain pen in perfectly straight lines.

Steve sits relaxed on his chair, sipping his coffee from a miniature white cup, his legs outstretched. He winks at me as if the procession in front of us is a staged entertainment event. He then glances at the young owner of the cafe and shrugs in bemusement.

'Well,' I say more to myself than anyone else, 'some Gnostic sources claimed it was Simon who was crucified, not Jesus, because they couldn't accept that Jesus was actually crucified'. And I leave it at that.

In the hotel we learn that our luggage is already on the way from Tel Aviv. A miracle of sorts. The Seven Arches Hotel is run by Muslim Palestinians who cater for Christian pilgrimages. In the lobby the waiting staff practise Christmas carols for us. What all politicians cannot resolve, tourism just might. In the Middle Ages, Jerusalem was believed to be the centre of the universe—it certainly used to be the spiritual centre of the western universe. I feel at more and more at home in this city—another scholar possessed with a passion for dangerous learning, possessed with a mania for understanding God.

Starved after the day of walking, we go straight to the dining room. One group of organised pilgrims is leaving and another arriving. In Jerusalem everything is a mirror and a reminder of what you are hiding or forging. Both groups of pilgrims are Polish. I wonder how I should relate to them after twenty years away from Poland. The first group is clearly made up of budget pilgrims from rural Poland. They sit, jovial and unselfconscious at the back of the dining room, stuffing oranges and other fruit into their pockets on their way upstairs to their rooms, as if they are still living under the martial law of 1981.

I remember during that time taking a train from Gdansk to my home town, Lublin. On the train I had my first experience of sensual delight. Someone on the train had an orange—a delicacy for the rest of us, as Poland was isolated politically and we had no access to imported goods. Oranges were one of those goods—exotic, tropical and forbidden. The scent of the peeled orange overwhelmed everyone on the train. It sank into our mouths, under our skin, into our eyes, with its glorious orange glow, full of fragrance. *A forbidden fruit.* I had licked my lips in the sweetest anticipation. That group of pilgrims is still stuck there, over twenty years later.

The new group is polite and whispers gently to each other, passing plates of food around. They get themselves better tables with a view of the city. Nobody ever said equality is the goal of a pilgrimage. At 4.30 pm we can see a golden haze setting above the city. The city looks sublime and surreally peaceful. It grows dark very quickly at this time of the year, but just before evening falls the city seems ethereal, as if all passions have calmed down and peace has descended on everyone.

On the way to my room I begin thinking about how in Jerusalem I have been experiencing strong, devotional emotions and I have been responding from my heart to places, people and fragments of Yeshua's life. Normally I operate mostly on an intellectual level. For years I studied philosophy of religion and theology. What's it all about? I would ask myself. There was a natural and guided interest there, but this was largely an intellectual exercise which had little, if any, transformative influence on me. Actually, it often caused an angry and rebellious response when I found the teachings too dogmatic or out of touch with human needs. Occasionally I would be charmed by some teachings, as I was with John Scotus Eriugena, a ninth-Century Irish philosopher accused of heresy. I loved his Neoplatonic vision of the universe as the fountain of creation. At times I would also become obsessively curious, as I did about St Augustine. His story was passionate and full of drama: a brilliant career or a service to God, a love for a woman or an ascetic life? The same thing later attracted me to the great Sufi poet, Rumi, and his take on the passionate aspect of our relationship with God. God as the Ultimate Lover. The Lover and the Beloved. But on the whole I couldn't relate to them except in intellectual terms. In Jerusalem my experiences are purely emotional, as if a space in my heart is rapidly filling up with devotion. In Toronto or Melbourne this space was either unavailable to me or dark. In Jerusalem I am experiencing the innocence of my heart.

THE TOMB: RETRACING THE STEPS

It has become a habit: we knock on each other's doors in the morning and come down for breakfast together. I like surrendering each day to Steve and Martin's plans and going along with them as the chronicler of an adventure. Sometimes I feel like a child guided and sustained by these two men. But most of the time I am a lost soul, clueless, searching for a new direction in life, with an enormous cloud of confusion over my head and nothing but an excruciating longing for something I cannot name. Whatever is meant to happen every day is entirely up to them and we discuss it over breakfast.

This gives me a sense of absolute spiritual splendour mixed with insanity. Martin has his plate topped with a mountain of scrambled eggs and sausages in front of him alongside a glass of orange juice. Steve and I have a cup of coffee each plus croissants with strawberry jam. Steve is half-listening to Martin's recollection of the trip from 2003, lost in his own thoughts, his face turned towards the magnificent view of the Old City. I love the city with the power of a new love. Steve is trying to decide whether he loves or hates it. He hates the political unrest and the part that the city played in the great drama of Yeshua's life. 'That's the city where he suffered', he often repeats as the three of us walk through the winding streets of Old Jerusalem and I sigh occasionally at their historical beauty. But Steve reluctantly loves it too and keeps coming back year after year, as if pulled by some invisible string.

'So you see, Joanna,' Martin talks to me from behind of the mountain of scrambled eggs, 'in November 2003 I came to Jerusalem for the first time. Like you, I got room 301 with the full view of Old Jerusalem, pulled a chair up to the window and thought, "That's it, I'm in paradise. I'm not moving away from this window for my entire stay in Jerusalem. Steve can run around making his discoveries. I'll stay here". I was dreaming of a lazy heaven when Steve walked into the room and proceeded to take me along on an unforgettable spiritual adventure. As we were walking out of the Seven Arches Hotel, I decided I would assist Steve in his search, "just in case it was God's will".'

I listen to Martin's story, wondering, *Isn't everything the will of God?* This question has puzzled theologians and seekers for centuries. Does God really require greatness from us, or is that just another delusion of the ego? I have had a strong ambition driving me for years. It has made me accomplish things and reach my goals, but ultimately it has also made me deeply unhappy. I have never been satisfied. Whatever I accomplish, I want more. First I found myself accomplished and unhappy. Then I was accomplished and broke. Ultimately I ended up accomplished, broke and alone. So I ask myself as I listen to Martin: 'Does God require greatness from us?' I have only the tiniest insight that, yes, God requires greatness from us—except perhaps this is not the greatness we have in mind. Can there be greatness aside from money, admiration, a slim body and (in my case) university degrees? Then I think, 'Maybe greatness on our part is in the adventure of meeting Him/Her/It? Isn't this being great?'

Steve turns back at us with expectation then gets up, knowing we will follow. We have an understanding that behind the story of the tomb we share the same thirst for a spiritual journey.

We leave the hotel immediately after breakfast and walk down the Mount of Olives again. The air is brisk and it is a beautiful sunny day. A strong smell of sweet incense comes to us from the Orthodox churches at the bottom of the hill. A smiling old Palestinian man, leading two camels, exclaims in English with great vigour, 'This is the day the Lord has made!'

We all laugh and feel energised.

Breathing the morning air, the three of us walk through the Lion's Gate and along the Via Dolorosa. Martin and Steve are anxious about the state of the site: whether it has been 'discovered' or damaged by anyone, whether the Department of Antiquities has claimed it. I can sense their anxiety, but I feel more my own excitement at being in this magnificent city that makes people mad with passion for God.

We follow the tiny streets through the Old City until we reach its other side at the Damascus Gate, so important to the story of Steve and Martin's discovery. At the Gate I inhale the sweet smell of oriental spices rising in the morning. These are the spices that were sought by the European kings and queens who sent ships in search of them, in the process bumping into the Americas, finding their way to India around Africa, and circling the globe. The spices were as important for European explorers as was their lust for new worlds. Now the old men sit quietly smoking their pipes, leaving the spices in all colours to seduce passersby with their fragrances.

Out on the street on the way to the Garden Tomb the Palestinians are selling fresh bread with holes in the middle like huge, flat doughnuts. Steve and Martin lead me to the Garden Tomb—known as the Protestant Tomb as it is on the way to the tomb they discovered. It is, they tell me, really well excavated and gives a good representation of how Yeshua's tomb possibly looked in the first century. Strictly speaking there are three tombs in Jerusalem that claim to be *the* tomb in which the body of Yeshua was left after the crucifixion. The tomb in the Holy Sepulchre is the first one and is supported by the Catholic and various Eastern Orthodox Churches. The Garden Tomb is the second one. Steve and Martin's discovery is the third.

The Anglicans believe that the second tomb, also called the Garden Tomb, is the alternative to the Church of the Holy Sepulchre. Like many other sites around Jerusalem, it has an interesting story behind it. In the nineteenth century General Charles George Gordon (1833-1885) came to Jerusalem to rest between the wars he was fighting for the British Empire. I'm not sure how the Sudanese or Chinese feel about him, but at that time the British considered him a hero. Gordon Pasha (as he was called) loved Jerusalem and often stayed in the American Colony to meditate, study the Bible and admire the great views of the city. One day, as he was sitting on a roof of the American Colony building overlooking the city, he noticed a hill which looked like a human skull. This was important, as *Golgota*, the hill on which Yeshua was crucified by the Romans, means 'the skull'.

General Gordon was convinced he had found the real Golgota and that the other Golgota in the Holy Sepulchre had been wrongly identified. His problem with Golgota being located inside the Holy Sepulchre, as identified by the Church, was that it was a very small, steep and solid rock. The Romans were excellent engineers with practical minds; they looked for logical solutions to problems, sometimes even gruesome ones, such as finding an efficient way to kill criminals and rebels. The soil on the hill had to be soft and easy to drive crosses into, on account of the mass executions they held for the rebellious Jewish population of their empire. Anyone who disobeyed them in any way or defied their perception of *Pax Romana*, the 'Roman Peace' of sharing gods and Roman laws, was crucified. And thousands of people were crucified in each rebellion. The Golgota of the Holy Sepulchre would not have fulfilled their criteria. The other problem was that, according to all sources, the tomb had to be located in a garden, while the tomb in the Holy Sepulchre is located in a rocky area right by a quarry. All the sources, the Bible and the Gnostic Gospels alike, say that on the day of the resurrection Mary Magdalene went to a garden, not to a stone quarry, to anoint the body of Yeshua. When she saw a stranger, she immediately took him to be a gardener (as you would expect in a garden) and not a rock polisher. But Gordon could not do much about his discovery: soon after returning to Sudan he died in Khartoum. Yet his idea survived. Doubt about the traditional Golgota persisted, and when a tomb was found in the area it was established as an alternative to the Holy Sepulchre and named the Garden Tomb.

The Garden Tomb is a beautiful, peaceful enclave in the midst of the delirium of the Old City. There is serenity here, and the people who volunteer here, including our guide Greg Wolfe, a young American expatriate, do a wonderful job of preserving the place and telling the story of its discovery. The volunteers don't claim this to be the true tomb of Yeshua; rather, it is one of the possible sites and, if nothing else, a memorial. The strongest argument against the Garden Tomb comes from archaeologists who agree that the tomb located here is from the first kingdom period and, consequently, is too old to be Yeshua's tomb. The New Testament was adamant that the tomb in which the body of Yeshua was put to rest was a new tomb for the family of Joseph of Arimathea from the second kingdom period.

I like the Garden Tomb but don't feel any moving experience here. Can this be an indication of anything? The place is more 'natural' and probably closer to the description of how it might have been in Yeshua's time: a quiet garden, not far from the Damascus Gate. It is also more natural in comparison to the Holy Sepulchre with its great architecture and history of the Crusades. The Holy Sepulchre, filled with fervently praying pilgrims and curious-if-polite tourists, is imbued with a sense of greatness, of complicated histories entangled in every stone. There is very little peace or any feeling of how it was back then. But the Garden Tomb has that. It has that peace. And a sense that, yes, it probably looked this way when Yeshua's body was brought here to rest by his followers, who included the wealthy man to whom the garden and the tomb belonged. The Garden Tomb seems a beautiful reconstruction of that moment, rather than the place itself.

I walk through the Garden looking for Yeshua's presence, leaving Steve and Martin to ask the guide detailed questions. I go back to the tomb itself, with its off-white walls, its two chambers, and carved stone 'beds'—as if they were meant to last for eternity. One of the bed-like places where the bodies were laid even has a pillow carved out of the stone. *The living taking care of the dead.* A much nicer way to be laid to rest than modern cemeteries, don't you think? I look again at the tomb and its chambers, but Yeshua isn't there. Not for me, anyway. It doesn't even matter much that many archaeologists believe the tomb is too old to be Yeshua's tomb. He is just not here.

If the Garden Tomb is the first challenge to the claims of the Holy Sepulchre, then Steve and Martin's discovery is the second. We retrace their experience from two years earlier. I allow them to lead me there, step by step, as they tell the story of their tomb. I have been waiting for this moment since we met in that cafe in Richmond, where they showed me the photos of the rock ledge in the middle of Jerusalem and told me it could be Yeshua's tomb.

Back in 2003, Martin and Steve arrived in Jerusalem very early in the morning and went to visit the Garden Tomb. There were already two possible tombs in Jerusalem then: the Church of the Holy Sepulchre and the Garden Tomb. Steve's idea was to make measurements as outlined in *The Urantia Book* and check which of the tombs accorded better with the measurements. They left their luggage in the foyer of the Seven Arches Hotel at about five o'clock in the morning and walked down the Mount of Olives across the Kidron Valley, then up to St Steven's Gate and along the Via Dolorosa. Near the Damascus Gate a small group of women ran past them. No one else was around.

'How strange', Steve thought, as it reminded him of descriptions of the Easter event when the women who went to anoint Yeshua's body ran away from the tomb when they saw a man standing there and took him for a ghost. According to *The Urantia Book*, the women then ran towards the city through the Damascus Gate. This recollection encouraged Steve to move forward and investigate the possibility of the tomb on the other side of the Damascus Gate as he read in the book.

Steve and Martin continued up to the Garden Tomb which General Gordon had located. But it was still closed due to the early hour. As they waited, they decided to follow the measurements from the book and see where the tomb might be. They sat on a bench near a newsagent's shop with a map and reflected on the exact descriptions of the tomb in the book: the tomb faced east, covered approximately one hundred square feet, was hewn out of rock, and lay along the Damascus Road. Steve was determined to find it. Based on the information in *The Urantia Book*, he estimated that the tomb should be about five hundred to a thousand metres north of the Damascus Gate. He said to Martin, 'The way the topography is and the way we are going, I think the tomb should be around eight hundred metres north of the Damascus Gate and, in order for it to face east, according to the layout of the land it would have to be that way'. As they moved down the street jumping over fences, they came across an Eastern Baptist church where a small group of people were conducting a service. They invited Steve and Martin over for a cup of tea. One of the men, who had lived in that area for over thirty years, began chatting with them.

Steve asked him, 'Do you know of any solid rock around here, somewhere near where the land slopes down?'

The man said, 'Yes, you're almost there', and gave them directions on how to get there. They looked at the map, looked at the compass, and followed the man's directions. They then walked around and around but couldn't see it. Steve calculated that from that point it had to be within two hundred metres. Then they saw a small footpath leading to a plot of barren land. This island of empty land right in the middle of Jerusalem had not been developed by anyone and was being used temporarily as an unauthorised garbage dump! Only a short walk away from the American Colony Hotel and a major intersection. Martin took the low footpath, while Steve walked across the rocky area with his compass pointing east. He soon came to a ledge. Within minutes Steve was standing on top of the ledge while Martin was standing next to the ridge, pointing. Steve looked down only to realise he was standing on top of rock about a foot thick. He peered over, cleared all the garbage from the top of the rock and saw an opening, almost completely buried, running in a straight horizontal line across the rock. This was too precise and straight to be a natural opening; it had definitely been constructed. All they knew at that stage was they had found something like a cave and that it was not natural—it had been carved out of the rock. They could see chisel marks matching descriptions from *The Urantia Book*. Steve crawled in on his belly. When he reached the rear of the cave and tried to feel the corners he found that the edges were perfectly rounded; all the lines of the cutting met in a beautifully rounded form.

He came out and said to Martin, 'This might be it!'

It would be a year before they returned. During that time they tried to find out how to excavate the area without causing an upheaval, who owned the land, and whether it was possible to excavate there or even buy the plot. Before this could be done they would have to clear the rubbish and have a closer look at the site. On their second trip in 2004 they brought a shovel with them. I loved the story: two Aussies travelling to Israel with a shovel! But their naive idea didn't work as the debris inside the site was too compacted and it would have taken a team of people to extract. Soon after, Steve and Martin derived another clue from the description in the book about the area of the tomb itself. According to *The Urantia Book*, the tomb was supposed to be about one hundred square feet in size. Steve crawled inside the site with a tape measure. From corner to corner the tomb measured 99.5 square feet. Near the tomb they noticed a cistern, which suggested the area around it used to be a garden. This made perfect sense to them—the area was called the *wadi*, or valley, and water naturally runs through the centre of a valley. A perfect place for a garden.

Martin tells me the story as we walk from the Garden Tomb towards the site, but I can't concentrate on the details. I try to imagine it as we walk through a densely populated Palestinian area, with small shops and a number of Christian churches that have been here for centuries. When we turn to the left and go down the street all we see is a large empty stretch of land covered with nothing but dry grass growing there and small piles of garbage. 'Now it's my turn to see it', I keep thinking, as Steve points at a small ridge in the middle of a garbage pile: 'Here!'

I am too overwhelmed to know what I feel. I can't think of this as anything other than a site. To think of it as a tomb is too much right at this moment. I want to protect my sanity; I want to obey the sceptical voice within which will allow me to feel doubtful and superior.

'Isn't it concrete?' I ask with doubt, pointing at the edge of the claimed tomb. A part of me desperately wants to participate in this, but the intellectual in me is looking for reasons to discredit the validity of this desire.

'No', Steve replies. 'We checked it. It's solid rock.'

We examine the site thoroughly. The Department of Antiquities hasn't claimed it as yet, but the area has definitely been cleared up a bit and is probably being used as shelter or storage for a homeless person. The ledge is uncovered and someone has clearly dug deeper into a niche-like space inside and made themselves a temporary door from a dark brown rusted roll of metal. On the other side of the road we can see police cars and the police questioning several Palestinian men. Steve cautiously takes a few pictures of the site while Martin and I sit on the ledge surveying the ancient panorama of the city.

I jump off the ridge and look inside the cave-like site. It is filled with rubbish. I go down on my knees and carefully crawl deep inside.

'Can you see an arch there?' Steve yells.

I look at the back wall of the cave. The lack of light and the rubbish are obstructing my view, but I can discern an arch at the side of the wall. I check again.

'Yes, I can see it!' I yell back. I look around the place again to contemplate what it might be—to study the essence, the motive of our spiritual adventure. I slowly crawl back to the surface; Steve and Martin are crouching at the entrance.

We walk in silence, or perhaps we talk—I don't know. We might be babbling in excited voices. I only know that I can feel my heartbeat in my throat. Steve and Martin are probably discussing different options for action, but I am dealing with feelings which have completely overwhelmed me. 'It could be his tomb and I have just entered it', I keep repeating silently in my mind.

Just as they did in 2003, we too go to the American Colony Hotel for a drink in the bar. Martin turns to me with his glass of wine and says, 'If you pinned me down and asked me, "Do you think we've found the tomb of Jesus?" my answer would be yes, qualified by the fact that there is a little bit of archaeology which could disprove it'.

'For example?' I ask.

'First, it needs to have a groove near the entrance on which the stone closing the tomb would rest. It was a large stone which was a sort of door at the opening of the tomb. To get in or out someone strong would have to push the stone and roll it along the groove. The groove was there to facilitate the moving of the stone. That will be a definitive marker as it is described in most sources.'

I listen to him, thinking, 'Why would you even think of looking for the tomb in a different place than the one established by tradition?' You'd have to be an Aussie to think like that, and I'm not Aussie enough. The traditional tomb is supposed to be in the Church of the Holy Sepulchre. Imagine what people will think: 'Oh yeah? Two Aussies came along and rearranged all the Christians' pilgrimage sites that had been venerated in the same places for nearly two thousand years, huh!' Yet the body of archaeologists generally doesn't agree about the Holy Sepulchre. Some think it is the site of Yeshua's tomb, some don't. A mass of doubt exists. The case for the Church of the Holy Sepulchre is almost entirely based on tradition. When Steve said to Martin, 'Let's look for the tomb as indicated in *The Urantia Book*; let's see if we can find the site matching the clues', they didn't intend to look for the 'true' tomb, but for a tomb matching descriptions from the New Testament and *The Urantia Book*. As far as Steve and Martin's site is concerned, it corresponds to a great number of clues in the book. But there are still other indicators to check. The most critical one being the groove at the bottom for a large rolling stone door.

In the evening back in my hotel room I think about what Steve and Martin have told me about their sources and I begin my own search through sources. First I look through the four gospels in the Bible—the official version of events. I sit on my bed taking notes in my journal as I read. In the Bible, the story is told in four different ways in the Gospels Matthew, Mark, Luke and John. All the gospels, both the canonical and Gnostic ones, were written long after Yeshua's crucifixion—most likely by the next generation of followers of the disciples who knew Yeshua in person. Estimates differ, but the time gap between Yeshua's crucifixion and the gospels was roughly forty to seventy years. This is not unusual. Yeshua didn't write anything himself. His disciples did—the best they could—and sometimes with their own agendas in mind, their own memories or the recollections of others, to preserve the teachings. In the case of Matthew, Mark, Luke and John, it is almost undisputed that their gospels were not written by them personally but by disciples. Each of these gospels carries the flavour of a person retelling a story as it was passed on to them. In each version of the story it is Mary Magdalene (in some versions accompanied by other women) who sees the resurrected Yeshua first. And in all the gospels, neither Mary Magdalene nor the disciples recognise him initially.

The Gnostic Gospels often talk about the meeting of the risen Yeshua in a different form, stressing that he was not of the same body. The Gospel of Mary Magdalene is one of the most abstruse on the matter. As the male disciples despaired after their Teacher's crucifixion, Mary Magdalene spoke to them and asked them to relinquish doubt and allow Yeshua's grace to guide them. Peter turned to her and said, 'Sister, we know that the Teacher loved you differently from other women. Tell us whatever you remember of any words he told you'. Mary Magdalene then explained how she saw Yeshua in a vision and asked him what the nature of this apparition of him was. Yeshua responded that he was neither in the spirit nor in the soul but between these two states (page 10, lines 23 and 24). *The Urantia Book* gives a slightly less enigmatic interpretation, claiming that after the resurrection Yeshua was in an intermediate state between bodily flesh and the spirit. Hence, his disciples did not recognise him until he spoke.

I place the Bible, the Gospel of Mary Magdalene and *The Urantia Book* on the coffee table by the window, turn off the lights and go back to bed. My mind is preoccupied with what I have read, but is unable to process it. The horrific spectacle of Easter processions with a tormented man-God on his way to a cruel death is gone. Instead, a great mystery is being born. I am much more comfortable with this mystery. This is a spiritual puzzle I am not going to solve. The only important thing for me is to start anew: a new relationship, a new love, a new friendship with Yeshua. Without hang-ups. Without bad memories and insistent dogmas. They are all gone. It is all gone. But I can't fall asleep. My mind can't stop asking questions.

What about the history of the tomb—the full story? Is our search similar to that of Helena's, Constantine's mother? Hers is also a detective story. Perhaps it was a little easier for her, as she came to Jerusalem three centuries after Yeshua's crucifixion. We are here two millennia later. She began her search in the fourth century by talking to people, asking about any living traditions, any memory of the events from Yeshua's life. Even in Helena's time, this was already a great operatic drama overlaid by other historical dramas. I want to honour her story too. It is too easy to believe of her as simply the ambitious mother of the new Emperor of Rome. Constantine prayed to the Christian God for victory over his enemies and promised that if he won, he would convert to Christianity. And here she was on a mission to Jerusalem to fulfil her son's promise. The events of recent years have stripped me of my intellectual pride and armour. I have to accept that the desire for intimacy with God, with the divine, with whatever or whomever you want to call that great power within us, had been driving me and pushing me to prioritise it in my life, even if only for a brief time. Why deny Helena the same driving force?

As an empress and the mother of the emperor, she had nothing to prove. Her trip to the Holy Land was not a sideshow or some hobby to give her time away from the palace. She was driven by the same desire to know the earthly side of Jesus. I imagine Helena as a fascinating woman with lots of courage, a wise woman with some luck, which allowed her to survive the vicissitudes of political and religious life in the great empire. She came to Jerusalem when she was nearly eighty to find exactly what Steve, Martin and I are looking for: traces of a great being called Jesus, Yeshua, the Son of God. If I were to meet Helena, I would ask her about the difference between the essence and the drama of life, about truth and the creation of truth, about seeking and finding, about the illusion of everyday success.

'Why are we so obsessed with personal and historical dramas?' I would ask her. 'Why aren't we happy with the eternal meaning from the teachings of great beings like Yeshua? Why do we crave meeting them on a personal level? Why seek Yeshua and his artefacts instead of being happy with the Jesus we were given?' Perhaps because we are creatures of time, and time creates stories. There is no drama, no simple or complex story of birth, life, redemption, enlightenment, evil and good, without time. In eternity everything is now. God is now. You are now. That is why we are One with God in eternity. That is why heaven, whatever it is, must be in eternity, because eternity equals union with God. The eternal now. The elusive now, right under the skin of time, under the life of every human being, underlying each drama, each event, personal or historical. It is there, the eternity we seek, the union we seek. The union that will end our suffering and our search. But we always get lost in the search and, yes, I freely admit I enjoy this search, the hide-and-seek with God, because I want to find God in my own unique way. How human, to want that.

I fall asleep. In my dream, I see a group of women rushing through the city before dawn. They pass the Damascus Gate and go into a garden containing a family tomb belonging to their friend. It is still dark when they arrive in the garden. They are a little scared, looking at each other, trying to find the courage to do their duty and anoint the Teacher's body. They feel that something is wrong, that this visit to their Teacher's tomb is different from other times when they have gone to visit deceased relatives and parents. Perhaps they believe the strange prophecy that their Teacher will be resurrected. Perhaps they are afraid to face the tomb in case he isn't resurrected. Secretly they hope he will be there in body. That his body will be there so they can take loving care of him. Their beloved Teacher. One of them, Mary Magdalene, approaches the tomb. She walks up very close then turns her face to the women standing a few steps away and says very quietly, 'The stone has been moved'.

The women cry in disbelief: 'They've stolen his body! They stole the Teacher's body!'

Mary Magdalene walks into the tomb. It is empty. She stands there for what seems like an eternity and returns to the panicked women.

'He is gone', she says, again very quietly.

With her eyes, I see the women run towards the city gate. They run through the Damascus Gate as the sun is slowly rising above the sky. They run as if propelled by a great power. *Wings on their arms. Flying through the Damascus Gate.*

Mary Magdalene sees it all, standing alone in the garden, transfixed by love. She turns her head as she sees the shadow of a man standing to her left.

'He must be a gardener', passes through her mind. Like a ghost herself, she moves in the direction of the man until she faces his back. 'A strange gardener', she thinks. 'Not doing anything, just standing there.'

Another thought enters her mind almost involuntarily, 'He is waiting for me.'

'Gardener,' she asks, 'Have you seen what happened to my Teacher?'

The man turns to her and says very softly, in a voice she can never forget, 'Mary, do you not recognise me?'

I wake up before dawn in the darkness of my tormented, confused soul. I lie in bed until the sun rising above the city elevates me. The sublime in me rises with the sun—or is it that the city at that moment is revealing its entrancing divinity? A wonderful peace settles in my heart with the sweetest joy, before the new passions, new pain, new jealousies and confusion will besiege me during the day. Yet at the moment the sun rises above the Old City sublimity pervades, despite all the guilt, misunderstandings, competitiveness and confusion of the old religions.

Yahve, Mohammed, Yeshua, Mary Magdalene. This is Jerusalem for me—the mirror of the human soul.

MARY MAGDALENE

It is only our third day in Jerusalem, but it seems like we have been here forever. We have one more day before we will go to Tel Aviv to meet with lawyers as our meeting is scheduled for our fourth day in Jerusalem. We are anxious about the lawyers even if we don't mention them just yet. There will be plenty of time tomorrow to be aghast with anticipation of their reaction. Will they laugh at us? Will they agree to assist us in claiming the land and proceeding with the excavations? All of these questions are on our minds. On an emotional level, nothing feels more natural or more eternal than walking from the Seven Arches Hotel down the hill: the Mount of Olives, the same Mount of Olives that Yeshua and his followers walked. *How did it feel to walk that hill with him?*

As you walk that hill you turn into a pilgrim, whether you want to or not. You are a pilgrim. You think he must have been a strong man to walk incessantly about this land, teaching. You make a joke about the healthy thighs they all must have had, including the women who followed him more faithfully than any man, the women whom for two thousand years organised Christianity did its best to discredit. The women who

63

listened to him, cooked for him, cared for him, loved him and who stayed with him when everybody else had left him. The sources differ on the number of women disciples. The most commonly mentioned names, apart from Mary the Mother and Mary Magdalene, are Martha, Joanna, Salome, Rachel and Rebecca. Some of them were poor, some were wealthy, aristocratic women—like Joanna, who was the wife of an official at the court of Herod Antipas. And here you are—a woman who, through a bizarre set of circumstances, is walking down the Mount of Olives, thinking how strange that this has happened when you had stopped believing in it all, were tired of old stories that did not make sense.

So we walk down the hill passing the churches—too many to mention, too symbolic to forget. We stop by the Russian Orthodox church of Mary Magdalene, with its golden domes like the ones you can see in Russia. It is not often open for visitors.

Opening Hours: Tuesday 10 to 12. Steve reads the sign on the closed door of the fortress-like surroundings. He has been there before on his previous trips, and in a musing tone he tells us how he met 'a pretty young nun' there once who 'shared the story of her life before the convent' with him. 'She was quite wild when young', he concludes whimsically. I catch myself feeling vaguely jealous.

The church was built by a Russian Czar, Alexander III, in memory of his mother—a sign that Mary Magdalene enjoyed a much more privileged position in the Eastern Orthodox Church than in the West. Both the church and convent are completely enclosed behind high walls. The whole complex is surrounded by small cottages of rough rustic beauty. We guess that the nuns live there. I imagine they come from south of the Ukraine, from villages near Odessa. Inside the church we see some of them. I would like to detect traces of Mary Magdalene in them, but I can't. The ascetic darkness of their habits betrays their young bodies and makes them appear mysterious and caught in some longing only devotion can appease. They are much younger than women in western convents, where one sees only remnants of old faith. The young nuns dressed in black move noiselessly among the altars of the church, lighting the long, thin Russian church candles. I sit in front of the altar on the right side of the nave and watch them as if they are creatures from another time.

At the centre of the main altar I notice a big painting of Mary Magdalene giving an egg to the Emperor Tiberius. There is a power in this image: a bold offering to an emperor by a legendary woman whom Yeshua is said to have kissed on the lips, causing jealousy amongst the apostles. I don't care for Christian interpretations of this symbol. I want to find my own meaning in this image, an image of new life. The story is rich, colourful and audacious. It emanates power and wisdom and is a great story of love and transformation, of the feminine I long to live. How would it be to follow a great being and love him as a woman, then be completely transformed by that love? Beyond possessiveness, jealousies and the worldly aspects of love? And to choose an even more magnificent love for the gift of peace and wisdom. 'My Peace, I give unto you', Yeshua said to his disciples. The peace of a more profound vision of life, seen and lived as a continuous beatitude.

As I sit in front of the altar I remember attending a graduation mass in my mid-twenties at St Michael's Church at the University of Toronto. I was being awarded a medal for the best philosophy graduate of the year. My mother had come from Poland to be present at the ceremony. She was very proud of her daughter, who hadn't spoken English until high school but had continued her studies in Canada at an English-speaking university. That was my mother's dream: to have an educated daughter. It was also my dream, except that my dream was spiced with the desire for adventure—the exotic and the other. Anything outside of Eastern Europe made for a potential exciting other. I didn't want to just earn a degree; I wanted a degree in another country, in another language, in an esoteric discipline of the philosophy of God. That was my learning adventure.

I had left Poland to begin my journey of discovery. But at St Michael's Church I had felt no ease, no sense of completion or satisfaction. There I watched one row of good Catholics after another going to the altar, queuing in front of the priest to receive Holy Communion, and I couldn't move. Sweating and embarrassed, I sat there like an outcast, overwhelmed by guilt because I was a *sinner*: every student in the church went to communion except me. The terrible sum of my sins consisted of living in a de facto relationship with a Canadian man (and communist)—a relationship not sanctioned by the Church. How was it possible that a young woman, who at nineteen had emigrated on her own, who spoke several languages including Latin, who studied medieval manuscripts and was planning in her own naive way to conquer the world of knowledge, could feel that way? Feel unworthy of participating in a religious ritual supposed to remind people of the teachings of a great being?

Years have passed since that moment and I have moved miles away from Catholicism and the messages of sin and unworthiness the Church so efficiently passes on to its faithful. Beyond the two thousand years of tradition, the great thinkers and saints, the fancy garments of bishops and cardinals and magnificent art sponsored by the popes. Beyond the messages most Catholics receive from their Church which are: 'there is something fundamentally wrong with you', and 'you were born a sinner because of original sin, Adam and Eve, the apple and the snake'.

If there was one 'sinner' who captured the Catholic imagination more than anyone else it was Mary Magdalene. It is no coincidence Mary Magdalene represents a sinner in Christianity. Depending on what sources you choose to read, she was a sinner, a prostitute, an adulteress, or an apostle. Although the rationale of unworthiness goes back to the idea of original sin, the concept of sin has always been connected with sexuality. What did Adam and Eve do in Paradise that was so wicked it led to their expulsion? It had something to do with disobedience, temptation and transgression. Centuries of Saints and theologians discussed the possibilities. What was the real business behind the forbidden fruit, and who was Mr Snake?

For ages, tradition portrayed Mary Magdalene as a prostitute. Was it just the simple male fantasy of a beautiful sinner saved by Grace? The story itself probably wasn't true. Two apostles (Mark 16:9 and Luke 8:2) describe how Yeshua expelled seven demons from Mary Magdalene, but nobody seems to know what this means. Hindu-inspired interpretations suggest the episode was in fact an awakening of *Kundalini* energy in her seven chakras, and a transformational experience in which all past negative tendencies could be expelled. Who knows?

In 591 CE Pope Gregory announced that Mary Magdalene and a nameless prostitute mentioned in the Gospel of Luke were one and the same woman; this was accepted as true for centuries. I was surprised to discover as a student of medieval philosophy and theology in Toronto that in 1969 the Catholic Church quietly admitted the lack of evidence in the Bible connecting Mary Magdalene to the prostitute. So why did the perception of Mary Magdalene as a beautiful-yet-sinful temptress remain in the public imagination? The perpetuation of this image would not have proved so effective over the centuries if the interpretation wasn't somehow attractive to us. Did it survive because it was an exciting way of telling young Yeshua's story? Having a repentant, seductive sinner, a beautiful ex-prostitute, in his entourage?

Joseph Campbell, a great writer on myths and their power in our lives, believed that the mythical figures of our culture are embedded somehow in our deeper consciousness, that often we subconsciously inherit or accept a prevalent myth and live it, even if it makes us miserable. The clue to a happy life, he said, was to consciously choose our own myths so we can live the life we want to live, rather than carry on unconsciously fulfilling the social expectations around us. What is my archetype? I want to be powerful, wise and seductive. I want to be spiritual, creative and radiant. I want all of that, yet I do not feel empowered as a woman. I have always felt I was a girl, not a woman.

As a young woman I wanted to lose my virginity so I could become a real woman. I needed the sexual ritual, the sexual bonding with an 'other' who was completely different from me— not only physically, but mentally and emotionally. I craved these differences so I could identify myself against them. Perhaps it was because I grew up among women, I don't know. I longed for that presence of another, a man—not to lose myself in him or worship him, but to know myself through him, so he could be my *telling mirror*. I longed for a man in the wicked, provocative manner of a young woman curious of her powers, wanting to unleash her sexuality and test its impact. I wanted to be empowered by my sexuality and was drawn soon enough into the paradigm of seductress and the transgression of sanctioned, permissible love. I didn't know then that a seductress always lives within the fantasy men create about her and is kept busy sustaining that fantasy so men continue to desire her. In the end she is always trapped by the desire to be desired. I didn't know then that being desired did not intrinsically create devotion and love. It generated more desire, more passion, more bondage, until the cycle wore itself down in emotional exhaustion. That knowledge, that experience, came many years after my graduation—after I left Toronto to live in Malaysia then in Melbourne. After several complicated relationships with complex men. When the seductive question 'How could he resist me?' transformed into the knowledge that 'Just because he might not be able to resist me doesn't mean he will give me what I want.'

It was only years later, while living in Melbourne and no longer even remotely connected to the Catholic Church, that I found my way back to the Gnostic Gospels. Surely I had heard something about the Gnostics when studying at the Pontifical Institute in Toronto? They had always interested me—the controversial and mysterious early Christian dissenters who thought they could interpret the gospels without the Church's help. The Church persecuted them slowly and efficiently throughout the centuries and burned them as heretics. The first time I heard about them was while writing my Masters thesis on St Augustine, a charismatic genius of Late Antiquity. I had been fascinated by him since reading his biography by Peter Brown (1969). Augustine fired up my medieval imagination. Perhaps because I was an intellectual snob back then I liked the fact that Augustine was a sophisticated Saint. Not for him the kissing of lepers and helping of the poor on the streets. He was an ambitious young man who, like so many other men from the fringes of the Roman Empire, wanted to be a famous rhetorician in Rome. Yet he was an idealist and was looking for something more than a career to inspire his soul.

In Milan, his life was changed by sermons from another charismatic Saint and intellectual, Anselm. Augustine wanted to be more than just an orator praising the dubious achievements of the emperors and their bureaucrats—he wanted to teach the truth. There were complications, naturally, as he had a woman in his life—his beloved de facto wife—with whom he had spent about eighteen years and had a son. An inner power struggle manifested itself as he was to give his first important speech in Rome. At the very moment of what could have been his entry into a prosperous but empty career, he lost his voice. I loved that moment when the desire to look for a deeper meaning in life interrupted his more prosaic ambitions. In his memoirs, *Confessions*, he recalled that torment with the question: 'If not now, then when?' I didn't like what followed the incident. After much inner torment, he abandoned his lover/de facto wife to become a priest. This was not easy for him, as he was a passionate, sexual man.

Lust and sin preoccupied him for long periods of time. In his monumental work, *City of God* (which I read obsessively from beginning to end), he discusses lust and original sin in detail. We suffer from lust because of original sin, he concluded, while the ancient patriarchs of the Old Testament were in full control of their sexuality. Augustine wanted to believe that the ancient patriarchs could raise their penises at will, and only when they wanted to procreate. In retrospect I believe he was a complicated, intelligent man whom, to my detriment, I found irresistible. Later in his life, as Bishop of Carthage in North Africa, he was kept extremely busy fighting the Gnostics (who called themselves the Manicheans). The barbarians were at the gates of Rome, western civilisation appeared to be falling to pieces, the educated grieved the loss of the *Pax Romana*, yet Augustine celebrated the dawn of the new age which he hoped would bring triumph to Christianity. He was one of those brilliant and impossible men I just couldn't resist. My way of getting over him was to complete a Masters thesis on his writings about evil. This was quite an unusual obsession for a woman in her mid-twenties—to be wooed by a philosopher who had been dead for almost two thousand years.

But back to the Gnostics. Augustine fought them with his pen; I was spellbound by them. When Steve and Martin invited me to follow them to Jerusalem as a chronicler of their adventures, they asked me to read *The Urantia Book,* a modern-day Gnostic text. I liked parts of it, especially the chapters describing Yeshua's earthly life. There was one problem though—I found the descriptions of the spiritual universe too strange for my taste. Which was an odd reaction, because the esoteric visions of the universe (and its many layers inhabited by celestial beings of all kinds) had always been an integral part of most Gnostic texts. For me there was an ongoing problem with every inspired spiritual text: How do you reconcile the profound insights present in these texts with half-mad visions of far-away galaxies? Although *The Urantia Book* made interesting points about Yeshua's life, it didn't explain much about Mary Magdalene's past before she met Yeshua. In the book she is called Miriam of Magdala, a woman with a questionable past who joins other women following Yeshua on his mission. The 'questionable past' suggests some wickedness in Mary Magdalene's conduct before she met Yeshua. No details are given.

I am more interested in the traditional Gnostic Gospels written soon after Yeshua's death and forbidden by the synods of the Church. The Synod of Nicea in the fourth century allowed only four gospels to be chosen for the Bible: Matthew,

Mark, Luke and John. Other gospels were considered too controversial for the sensibilities of the bishops and church rulers. These gospels included the Gnostic Gospels, among them my favourites: the Gospel of Mary Magdalene, the Gospel of Thomas, and the Gospel of Philip.

Despite long centuries of repression, the Gnostic Gospels were unearthed one by one. The first of these was the Gospel of Mary Magdalene. It was found at the end of the nineteenth century in Egypt, then acquired by the National Museum of Berlin, and has been lovingly transcribed line-by-line, translated and popularised by the French scholar, Jean-Yves Leloup (2002). This gospel's earliest sections are as old as the so-called canonical gospels of the Bible. The most controversial lines of the Gospel of Mary Magdalene deal with the jealousy of the apostles at Yeshua's sharing of his teachings with her: 'How is it possible that the Teacher talked in this manner to this woman, about secrets of which we ourselves are ignorant? Must we change our customs and listen to this woman? Did he really choose her, and prefer her to us?'(17:9-20). According to Leloup, the anger of the apostles had nothing to do with Yeshua's personal relationship with Mary Magdalene. They were angry because he considered Mary Magdalene worthy of giving her 'his most subtle teachings' (2002, p.7). In doing this, Yeshua not only went against the traditional belief that women were unworthy of learning, but also let it be known that he treated her as equal to them. Despite her past, her transformation was complete.

But what sort of transformation was it? Surely not one which asked her to sacrifice sexuality for wisdom? I would hate to think she lost her sensual appeal after gaining wisdom and spiritual growth. I see her as she was presented in the Gospel of Philip in her resplendent sensuality, or as Leloup says, 'in the lively power of her sexuality' (2002, p. 7). The Gospel of Philip notes (59:9):

'Lord loved Mary more than other disciples, and often used to kiss her on her mouth.' I rather like the story of Yeshua kissing her—against all rules, against all proprieties.

This is how I see it: the morning sun reflecting brightly on the white stones of the synagogue in Capernaum; Yeshua's disciples standing around him, together with a curious crowd and some followers; and he just kisses her. He kisses her as she is standing in front of him in the glory of her beauty and the sensuality of her past.

Mary Magdalene was far more likely a young woman who had an affair with a married man. As far as we know, she never married, so it was unlikely she could have been unfaithful to anyone. She fell in love out of wedlock. Am I getting a little personal here? Many years after my graduation from St Michael's College, I had my own experiences of sexual transgression: a lengthy affair with a married man, to mention but one. What began as a one-night stand in the tropics turned into an addiction that lasted years and took me to Bali, Havana, Barcelona, Mexico and Australia. From the point of view of Mary Magdalene's story, I was no different from her. How does one move away from unsanctioned love, from a great passion that society forbids? Rumi, the great Sufi poet, mystic and lover wrote:

> *Lovers don't finally meet somewhere.*
> *They're in each other all along.*
> *Or even better,*
> *Wonderful. Go inside attraction.*

The idea that we can meet God in attraction, in passion, and merge with a beloved to become one with Him or Her in the act of love fascinated me, and I certainly practised it throughout my affairs (I even invented a word to describe my love relationships in detail—'tormentuous'). The spiritual dimension of sexuality is powerful and achievable, but extremely difficult to master. The biggest obstacle to mastering union with God through sexuality is attachment to the object of one's desire. If you can desire and, at the same time, be detached, if you can see God instead of a particular person, then you are a Sufi, a Tantrika, a great Mystic Lover. But I was addicted. Not just to particular men, but even more so to passion itself. I was addicted, so I suffered.

'Passion' comes from the Latin word denoting 'suffering' or 'being acted upon'. In troubadour poetry of the Middle Ages, 'passion' began to mean 'torment' or 'violent love'. Yet there were days, months and years in my life when the moments of ecstasy my passion gave me were worth all the suffering it brought, both before and after. There was an addictive element to passion I was reluctant to relinquish in the moments of aliveness, of fullness, of being that came between suffering and longing, between desire and the impossibility of its fulfilment, between what was 'right' and what was 'wrong'. Didn't Rumi say the space between the right and the wrong was where lovers met?

The mystical space of desire and the redemption of desire found Mary Magdalene and Yeshua in that historical moment where she was going to be stoned for a 'wrong' and Yeshua asked the eager crowd which one of them had not trespassed from the space of the 'right'. The tradition says he saved her. I would like to believe he saved more than her life. That itself would make a memorable parable, as one of the stories told about Yeshua's life. But it is much more seductive as a story of passion and love. The only thing that could transform Mary Magdalene was a higher love—a love so mysterious and sublime it could override the passion, desire, and addiction she felt for the other. On a personal level, we always need the other to strike the light; even the best match needs the surface of the other to ignite. Yeshua gave it to Mary Magdalene. *My Peace I give you.* The peace that will always stay with you. The peace that great beings of all religious traditions speak of. The peace of the enlightened. The peace of the Self. That peace is also love. Once Mary felt it, her life was transformed. Was she a prostitute? I don't think so. She was a woman of passion and strong desires. Passion for love in all of its guises. What makes you 'fall' can also make you 'rise'— these are relative terms that change our focus, move us in a different direction. The passion and desire which nearly brought her life to an end also raised her to the status of Yeshua's disciple and companion. Whether Yeshua and Mary Magdalene were sexually intimate or not seems irrelevant. Her passion uplifted her. Her love transformed her. From a sinner to a Saint. From passion to passion. This is Mary Magdalene for me.

We pass by Lion's Gate, enter the Old City again and, walking down Via Dolorosa, find the Basilica of Saint Anne. It is impossible to forget the stories of Jerusalem, where every stone is a symbol of something for someone. Saint Anne's Basilica is a symbol of the sublime feminine. Or is it? St Anne was Mary's mother—or so tradition says. The mother of the mother. In other words, Yeshua's nana.

My grandmother would often sit me on her knee and read books to me. She taught me how to read and count. A devout Catholic, she also tried to make me read about the lives of female Saints, while I hid in the orchard and read stories about the adventures of pirates. Did Anne straighten Yeshua's clothes before he went out of the house? Did she slap him when she thought he deserved it, or kiss him and embarrass him in front of other boys? Did she watch him—a studious, somewhat preoccupied boy—and worry about him? Did she hope he would become a great rabbi who would bring fame and honour to the family? Was she bitterly disappointed when he became a rebellious teacher, leaving her disgraced when he died as a criminal? We know nothing of his early years. But I like the idea of his closeness to his grandmother. The idea of a connection with women from his early years. From Anne to Mary to Mary Magdalene to Yeshua.

A family should be run by women. As a child I thought my grandmother, *babcia*, was the great matriarch, the giver of affection, the source of love, discipline and learning in the family. It was only later that my mum assumed that role when she told me which books to read. Both my grandmother and my mother lived the archetype of St Anne and Mary: the dutiful women, the wives and mothers. That archetype didn't work too well for my mother—she hated being a divorcee and had a daughter who had no intention whatsoever of making her a grandmother.

I see Steve coming back from the excavations next door to the church and wait for him to sit next to me on the bench.

'There is a beautiful feminine energy about this place', I say, more to myself than to him.

He sits down next to me. 'Yes, pure, unadulterated feminine.'

'Unadulterated?'

'Yes', he says. 'Non-threatening.'

How could the feminine be threatening to this man, I wonder, a man who has devoted his life to interesting, if eccentric, projects and seems so much in control of every aspect of his life? 'I have a complicated relationship with that energy. My mother was a wild child and I didn't see her much. My marriage . . . was a disaster.'

'You mean you were hurt?'

He looks at me, annoyed. 'I was *crushed*. Both times.'

'And what sort of feminine am I?' I press on.

As he does with everything else on this trip, he gives my question serious consideration. After a moment he says pensively, 'You are full-on feminine. When you're sad, you're tormented. When you're happy, you glow because you're so happy. You are full-on'. And as he says this he gets up to look for Martin, who is lost somewhere in the labyrinth of excavations. I stay behind, writing in my journal on the bench outside of the church: *The lines of lives intersect in simple moments. The past and the present. My mother, my grandmother, Steve's mother, Steve's ex-wife. Seductress, lover, wife. The parts we play.* A small reddish cat jumps on the wall behind me, sneaks under my arm and demands attention. 'You are full-on', I whisper in its ear.

THE LAWYERS

We take a taxi to the Central Bus Station near Jaffa Gate. An angry young Palestinian man overcharges us, and we get into an overcrowded taxi-mini-bus going to Tel Aviv. I immediately fall asleep (for exactly fifty-five minutes, according to Martin's count). In Tel Aviv we get off with everybody at a shopping mall where our bags are routinely checked by security. Martin calculates that we have about thirty minutes to spare, so we head off to a Moroccan food stand. We are served by a cheerful young Israeli girl who tells us that her family migrated from Morocco not long ago. 'What a strange place', I think. 'So ancient and yet nearly everyone you meet is a recent immigrant.' We eat too much: couscous and fish for me; chicken schnitzel, mashed potatoes and Coke for Martin; a chicken drumstick and rice for Steve. The girl who serves us has most of her underwear sticking out from her jeans. It has writing on it and I tilt my head to read it. The underwear's message is *Love. Pure.* I'm just as unkempt as on the entire first day of our trip when I walked around Jerusalem without my underwear (our luggage was lost), and now I notice a button is falling off my pants. The three of us leave the stall and run around the mall searching for a store selling needles and thread so I won't lose my pants in the lawyers' office.

To Steve and Martin's relief, I find the equivalent of a two-dollar shop with a huge collection of little boxes filled with threads and needles. I grab the closest one as Steve and Martin wave that the taxi is already waiting to take us to the lawyers' office.

The taxi driver asks: 'Where are you from?'

'Australia', we say.

'Nice country', he says, making a professional judgment. 'Where are you staying in Tel Aviv?'

'We're staying in Jerusalem', Steve says.

'Jerusalem?! Jerusalem?! What are you doing in Jerusalem?! There is nothing there but stones and bombs! Don't bother with Jerusalem! All trouble comes from Jerusalem! Come to Tel Aviv and sit on the beach! The stupid people in Jerusalem make shit economy in this country! All the conservative people there! What are you doing there? Here in Tel Aviv we are different! We have fun! We enjoy life! Stay in Tel Aviv!'

As we exit, I laugh and make him promise to wait; Steve and Martin keep suspiciously quiet. I still don't know what they are planning to tell the lawyers. I start to worry. I worry they will think we are lunatics.

'I'm sure they'll think we are lunatics', I lament as we wait for the lift. 'I worry if we should tell them . . .'

'That we are lunatics?' Martin interrupts. 'I'm sure they'll figure that one out!'

Steve starts to look nervous.

'No! About the site', I whisper to him in a conspiratorial tone. I turn to Steve. 'I worry that they'll charge you the full fee of $5000 US dollars! What are you going to do?'

'He'll pay', Martin says.

'I think they'll only charge me about a thousand US', Steve says quietly. 'No more.'

Fortunately the lift arrives and takes us to the offices, just as I am about to have a nervous breakdown.

The office is a spacious room furnished in a minimalist style. A long table takes up the centre of the room. There is plenty of space between us and them as we sit facing them across the table. You can't prevent some 'strategies' being played out when you know you are only a pawn.

Martin immediately helps himself to a large assortment of sweets and opens a bottle of juice for himself. The lawyers watch us like a silent army. There are three of them: Daryl, a Harvard-educated man in his late twenties who decided to move to Israel and follow the Orthodox path; Jacob, a muscular and masculine man who could easily pass for a professional boxer; and Oren, a young lawyer-in-the-making who assists Jacob.

I like Oren, an eager young man who, with every gesture, tries his best to make us feel comfortable and happy. In vain. I can hear my mind screaming, 'Oh my God! It will be revealed now to the world that we are three lunatics on some obscure adventure!' But once the idea of obscurity enters my mind, I calm down: for me, the obscure, the esoteric is homey and safe. I don't know how anyone else feels about it, but for me it is my safety zone.

The lawyers stare at us in expectation while Martin swallows a cracker and introduces me as 'an early Christian scholar', which makes me feel about two thousand years old. I worry I am not dressed properly for an early Christian scholar who is visiting BIG, EXPENSIVE LAWYERS. I worry that I look too sexy: my black pants are tight and my green blouse reveals flamboyant cleavage. How does one dress as 'an early Christian scholar' when visiting lawyers? In the meantime, Martin introduces Steve. Steve is not doing too well, is nervous and intense. His Aussie groove is completely gone.

'Do you know', he starts in a grave voice, 'that many professional archaeologists'—he puts stress on the word 'professional' as clearly none of us are—'contest the present site of Jesus' tomb?'

The lawyers try to look as if discussing the site of Jesus' tomb is a very ordinary exercise.

'On our last trip, two years ago, Steve and I discovered a site which we believe is possibly the place of Jesus' tomb', Martin says.

He shows them the pictures of the site. Jacob receives the pictures in an ironic, amused manner, as if thinking, 'Okay, so this afternoon we're meeting three Christian lunatics who believe they have discovered Jesus' tomb—as if there aren't enough crazed Christians visiting Jerusalem'. But he says, 'That entrance to the ancient *tomb*'—he stresses 'tomb' ironically—'is made of cement.'

Martin: 'No, surprisingly, it's not. We checked and it's made of stone, like tombs in the first century were.'

Jacob takes another look. 'Are you sure?'

Steve: 'Yes.'

Jacob passes the pictures to Daryl and Oren. To my relief, they look at them with interest.

Daryl: 'Interesting. Why don't you consult some Christian authorities instead of coming to a Jewish law firm?'

Do I detect more irony? As they chat I silently progress to the next stage of my nervous breakdown. Somehow I feel the legitimacy of our enterprise depends on this meeting.

Martin says, 'We don't think the Christian authorities would support a challenge to the established sites'.

Still examining the pictures in his hand, Jacob says, 'In Jerusalem, you can't kick a stone without thinking it might be an historical artefact. The Historical Society has a long list of sites to dig but little money. Very likely they'll say, "Let's keep the tomb under the ground where it's safe until money and time are available."'

Oren the young apprentice lawyer writes down everything with great vigour; I try to imitate him as I write down notes for our side. One would think we are in some competitive writing contest so future generations can decide whose interpretation of events is more correct.

Daryl is attentive, as if considering some secret agenda. He is a pale man with reddish hair and very intelligent eyes. Jacob is a pragmatic, solidly-built man. I'm sure he does exceedingly well in the boxing ring. He isn't hiding his amusement at our idealistic Christian enterprise—he has no time for any sort of esoterica. I take note of his focus and intensity and can sense his down-to-earth manly vitality, even though I wouldn't think him good-looking by any measure.

'Does it have anything to do with the Gnostic Gospels?' Daryl throws in casually.

I begin to relax and enjoy the show. 'Yes, Steve and Martin's discovery is based on modern Gnostic Gospels.'

With great gravity Steve passes a copy of *The Urantia Book* to the lawyers. Daryl takes it with respect and browses through it with interest. 'Is this a Gnostic text?'

'Yes, it's a modern Gnostic text. Martin and I made the discovery following descriptions from the book.'

Perfectly poised, Martin explains: 'It is an elaboration and expanded version of the gospels'.

Daryl asks, straight-faced: 'Does it contest any of the Catholic claims?'

Despite his strong Catholic background, Martin very calmly replies, 'Yes. Things such as the virgin birth, Mary's Assumption, etcetera'.

Daryl likes it. Oren scribbles something down very enthusiastically, and Jacob thinks it's too much fun to let pass.

Then comes what I am certain is the most divinely outrageous moment of the meeting.

'Who wrote it?' Daryl asks.

Martin, with a conviction I will never forget, replies: 'A number of celestial planetary beings. About thirty-three of them'.

The lawyers are still straight-faced. I pretend I've dropped something under the table so nobody can see my face. Martin spills his second bottle of orange juice. I spill my mineral water as I open the bottle. Steve is too tense to even open—let alone spill—anything. How do you explain to someone something you believe without sounding like an idiot? Especially religious texts and claims of supernatural sources? How can you take a scientific approach towards something based solely on faith?

Daryl relieves me of the self-conscious narrative running through my head by saying, 'Well, for your sake I hope you don't find the body there!'

I burst into laughter, point at him, and respond, 'Good one!' and we all start to laugh.

Steve interrupts seriously: 'I don't think that'll be the case as someone has already tampered with the site'. He points out to the lawyers the difference between the pictures taken yesterday and two years ago. 'You see there—that's the niche, now visible, which two years ago we only hoped would be there. You can see it because someone's uncovered it. We know it belongs to a *waqf*. Maybe the *waqf* had a look at it. We made a number of other predictions about the site and if they prove to be correct . . .'

Jacob studies the pictures with great intensity. Suddenly his energy changes. He gets up with unusual verve from his chair and says we need to immediately find an archaeologist to contact. I observe him as he becomes more and more energised and focused, as if he has surprised himself by deciding to join our team. He turns to Steve. 'Can you raise enough money for the dig?'

'Yes!'

I admire Steve's commitment and I am astounded by Jacob's shift as he moves about with increased energy and proceeds to make a number of phone calls, one after another. The ones I catch are to the Bureau of Antiquities, the Hebrew University, and a friend—a retired professor of archaeology. No doubt they'll help us. They'll help our mad, gnostic dream. I am melting. I see a big smile on Martin's face.

'It's all taken care of', Jacob says, visibly uplifted. He shakes our hands and gives an appreciative look at my inappropriate-for-an-early-Christian-scholar outfit. Then he runs off to another BIG LAWYERS' meeting while instructing young Oren to photocopy the relevant parts of *The Urantia Book*.

Suddenly the meeting is over. We all shake hands. I stick around Daryl and in my dazed state I charm him and babble something about my passion for gnostic texts and how marvellous it is that so many of them were rediscovered in recent years. Daryl tells Steve the first consultation is free, as Steve stands in front of him with a cheque book. I'm getting a ridiculous high. Meanwhile, Oren has already arranged for our transportation to the station. He walks with us to the taxi, takes us to the station, and tells us he'll leave soon for Cambridge to work on his Ph.D. Before we have a chance to catch our breath we are on the train going back to Jerusalem. I'm on such an ecstatic high that even Bernini's *Ecstasy of St Theresa* with her mystical orgasms would look mildly uninteresting in comparison.

The train leaves us in the modern part of Jerusalem, unfamiliar to us. It is already dark and much colder than in Tel Aviv. The weather in Tel Aviv was summer-like, but in Jerusalem it is all wind and cold. I button up my short black coat. My hair flies in the wind and I can hardly see anything.

We take a taxi to the American Colony Hotel. The driver is a man in his forties. He takes directions from us then calls his wife or girlfriend. The phone is on speaker. He isn't afraid that we will understand his Hebrew. We don't, but I am transfixed by the energy of the conversation. His voice is a hungry wolf's, wooing his prey. He speaks in a soothing tone, determined to conquer her in the sweetest possible way. Listening to his voice, I am convinced he has done this many times before. Then the woman talks in a husky, seductive way. Demi Moore would kill for that voice. I imagine they talk of love. They talk of sexual positions. They talk of their past sexual encounters, as lovers always do. About the agony of separation and the ecstasy of a new rendezvous.

'Schnitzel?' the woman asks in the huskiest of all voices, and he answers something in his hungry-wolf way.

'They're talking about dinner', I whisper to Steve.

'What?' Steve sounds like he has just woken from a distant dream.

'They're talking about their dinner plans', I whisper again.

'What's she saying?' Martin turns to Steve.

'Schnitzel!' I say triumphantly.

'What schnitzel?'

'I don't know. A type of food foreplay?' I improvise.

'Do you know what she's talking about?' Martin asks Steve again.

'I have no idea', Steve shrugs.

I opt not to mention the schnitzel anymore.

We walk into the American Colony Hotel like three mad dreamers. I insist on a feast. Steve leaves tips for everybody while I order an apple slice with pistachio ice-cream and red wine. Martin doubles my order. Steve chooses *crème brûlée* and white wine. Waiters ask if someone is getting married and we laugh.

I raise my glass of red wine and toast, 'To madness, courage and blind faith!'

At this moment, we feel guided by angels, anointed. We feel the whispers of wondrous helpers, a magnificent destiny all around us. Is it truth or are we deluded? In moments like these, it's best not to ask . . .

A couple of days later, Oren calls Steve and tells him Jacob has arranged for a meeting with an archaeologist, Shmuel Yaari. Steve becomes very tense and Martin is suddenly nervous. He walks around, moving his hands about his body as if performing some strange dance.

'Yes?' I ask, stunned by their response to the news. 'Isn't this good news?'

Steve sits down on the edge of the bed. 'I feel very protective of the tomb site.'

I sit down next to him, touch his arm, and whisper, 'Some things are preordained. This is what you wanted. Eventually you'll have to share this, even if it feels like full exposure'.

Martin is pacing around the room. Today I feel peaceful for both of them. Today they are too involved in the story to function with grace. Today I am the holder of peace.

We get ready within minutes. Steve hails a taxi as we stand outside the Seven Arches Hotel. It is the coldest day so far. The air is frosty and an icy rain falls on us. The wind changes the direction of the rain, all the time making it impossible to keep warm and dry. The taxi arrives. 'The Old Shamai Cafe', Steve directs the driver, who doesn't look too happy. Each time we order a taxi it is the same story. The Israeli taxi drivers don't want to go to the Palestinian parts of the city, and the Palestinian drivers are reluctant to go to the Israeli parts. The driver throws us out in front of the cafe and drives away as fast as he can. It is a large, two-storey cafe. We sit at a table on the second floor overlooking the rest of the cafe so as not to miss Shmuel.

He arrives. We recognise him intuitively; he looks like an old gentleman looking for someone. I like him from the moment we shake hands. He has deep, wise eyes. He is more than just an intellectual or an academic—he is a man who inspires trust.

'There are many tombs in that area from the Second Temple period, so it's possible you have found something of interest there.' His curiosity becomes aroused as Martin and Steve describe the details of the site. 'Do you think it is the tomb of a Saint?'

'This is what we think', Martin says very quickly.

Shmuel nods. His soft eyes smile. 'Often, local shepherds re-use the tombs as temporary dwellings for themselves and their animals. This could be the cause of the smoke on the walls of the cave.' He takes out a book from his bag. 'This is one of my books—my gift to you.'

I take the book from him and read the title: *The Historical Atlas of Jerusalem*. I pass it over to Steve.

'As a Jew and an outsider,' Shmuel continues, 'I can tell you that I don't believe the Holy Sepulchre is Jesus' burial place: it is within the walls of the city and crucifixions were not allowed within the city. They took place outside the walls. There are some claims that the city walls around Damascus Gate were different at the time of the crucifixion. Thus, there is a possibility that the place where the Holy Sepulchre is now was outside the city walls. But I do not consider these claims convincing'.

'They wouldn't bury people in the quarry either?' Martin asks anxiously.

'Occasionally they did bury people in the quarry because you can find carved-out places there. A convenient thing for poor people.'

'He was taken to a new tomb in the garden which belonged to a wealthy man, Joseph of Arimathea.'

Shmuel smiles. 'No wealthy man would have a tomb in the quarry.'

Oren arrives. 'Jacob might join us at the site.'

Once Oren is here, he mobilises us to go. Martin and Shmuel take one taxi while Oren takes Steve and myself in his firm's car with a driver from Tel Aviv who has never been to Jerusalem. The trip to the site is comical but long as we meander through the new parts of Jerusalem under the confused instructions of Oren—who does not know the city either. Oren pretends that this is all part of the plan and gives us an impromptu tour on the way to the site.

Finally we arrive. It is even colder now. We fight against the wind as we leave the car and walk to the site. In the distance we see Martin, Shmuel and Jacob talking by the site. I would give any amount of money to know what they are saying about it. The minutes between them, the site, and us, are unbearable. I want to know. I am sure Steve is in agony because of the delay. I want to know. Is it a tomb? And if it is, is it from the Second Temple period—a first-century tomb? My mind is driving me crazy. If the whole thing is a delusion, I want to know it now, so I can let go of the mystery. But do I really want to let go of the mystery?

Finally we are here. They look intense and focused. Jacob looks like he has had an epiphany. *Is it good or bad for us?* my mind screams at me. *I don't know!* I want to scream back.

'Well?' I ask, as Steve stands speechless behind me.

Jacob acts as if he can't be bothered with us anymore. His full attention is on Shmuel.

'Yes?' I repeat insistently.

'Be patient', Jacob says.

'Yes?' I'm not giving up, and position myself between Shmuel and Jacob.

'Yes, it probably is a first-century tomb', Shmuel smiles. Martin smiles. Oren Smiles. Steve collapses on the stones by the site. I feel I might faint like a Victorian lady. Instead I ask, 'Can I go inside and see what's there again?'

'Why not?' Shmuel smiles encouragingly.

I crawl inside on all fours. This time I can see better as more garbage has been removed. 'I can see a room carved in the rock', I yell at them. Shmuel bellows back questions about the details of the room and I answer them in the same way. As I am crawling back to the surface, Steve recovers, picks himself up, and takes a picture of me coming out of the tomb. I stand up, elated. Martin stays by Steve and Shmuel. Jacob is extremely possessive of Shmuel and doesn't leave his side even for a moment.

'So it's really it?' Jacob asks Shmuel again.

'It is, it is', Shmuel responds with his usual calm.

Steve is still dazed and wants to write Jacob a cheque for today's meeting, but Jacob doesn't seem interested—as if he is up to something much bigger than money this time.

Steve offers to pay for Shmuel's taxi back, but again Jacob waves him away. 'He is going with me', he says, and they both disappear.

I look questioningly at Oren.

'Jacob also has business with the Holy Sepulchre', he says.

'What?'

'The Holy Sepulchre has some real estate problems and Jacob is helping them.'

Despite my resolution not to faint, I am very tempted to do so. The Holy Sepulchre has problems with its real estate? My heart is beating wildly.

This city has its own wild beat too.

Which is probably why I love it.

BETHLEHEM

W e estimate that it will take us several days before the lawyers will contact us. There is nothing we can do until they investigate the necessary procedures about permits, excavations and even the very possibility of our plan. Meantime, I am eager to explore other facets of Yeshua's life and places where he was born, lived and taught. Steve, on the other hand, is eager to get away from Jerusalem and show me the other Yeshua, the child and the Teacher, not the suffering Christ. Martin is ready to go too. He feels a little wary of travelling and tired of the constant moving, but he too wants to go somewhere where the thinking about the possible actions of the lawyers is dimmed by new impressions. So we leave the Seven Arches Hotel. But Jerusalem is not that easy to leave behind. It is present in conversations with taxi drivers and everybody we meet. They carry the history of the city with them.

Jerusalem is the only place I know where the moment you meet people they immediately tell you their religion, their political stance and their nationality. Unasked. Religion, nationality and politics are so closely knit in Jerusalem that they have almost a medieval quality. They are people's stamp—their identity and their intense sense of belonging. The rest of the world seems to have lost such precise definitions of attachment, inclusion. We want to belong, but don't want to be smothered. It gives us comfort, but we place limits on it.

'Don't label me!' is my immediate response to people around the world who ask me about my accent or 'belonging'. For most of my adult life I have been fierce about not allowing people to categorise me, label me, according to their perception of what it means to be a person with this particular accent, that particular ethnicity or political stance. *Don't label me. I define who I am, not you.* And even more: *I can change allegiance any time I find something that engages me more.* This is the fierce independence I have cultivated. In Jerusalem it is the opposite: 'I am Charlie. I am Palestinian Christian. Do you need a taxi driver today? Where would you like me to take you?'

This is what Charlie says one morning when he approaches us as we are walking down from the Mount of Olives. He places himself very precisely and states his identity. Just like that. It could be that he sees us as some western tourists on the Palestinian side of the city and is offering his services. Maybe he is seeking some support from 'fellow Christians'. It makes me uncomfortable. I am not even sure how 'Christian' I am and how comfortable I am with identifying myself as one. I have come here to explore my relationship with Yeshua,— undoubtedly a great being—but I am not even willing to call him by his westernised name, Jesus, because that name seems so overused by people who I will never identify myself with (there is that word again—*identify*). I am definitely not comfortable (as much as Charlie is) being part of a 'Christian club'. Definitely not.

Once, as a teenager in Poland, I met a young man who had trained to be a priest. Bluntly, I asked him, 'Why?'

'Because I have met Jesus.'

His answer was a put-off for me. I judged him a freak and didn't feel like talking to him anymore. I was very young; I believed myself to be a philosopher and naively thought I was his intellectual superior. Some years later in Toronto I spoke about this exchange with a friend of mine who was a Zen Buddhist and he said with great delight, 'Wonderful! He connected with a great being and his teachings!' Still, I was puzzled—almost appalled. Probably because I assumed that the young man from Poland had 'met' a cheesy image of 'Jesus'—one of those popular representations of him as a tall, brown-haired, carefully coiffured man with a goatee, walking around talking about sheep and shepherds.

I want to have a relationship with that great being who has been influential in western culture, who lived a very dramatic life and whose teachings have often been twisted to support political and religious agendas. It is almost impossible to know exactly what he taught, but I want to know him personally—not belong to some fan club of whatever persuasion.

But Charlie knows exactly where he belongs and that this feeling has been passed on to him as a responsibility, however inconvenient. As soon as Martin, Steve and I get into his taxi, he lets us know.

I look sheepish. Steve sighs, 'Oh!' and Martin is very happy to hear more. 'So there are Palestinian Christians in Israel?'

'About two percent of the population in total', Charlie eagerly responds, starting his story as he manoeuvres the car out of the city. 'Nobody wants us here so people try to leave—but it is difficult to get visas.' He moves the fingers of his right hand as if trying to catch something beyond his grasp. 'We are squeezed between the fighting Muslims and Israelis. We are too small to matter to anyone. Generally the Israelis want us to leave, but the Church wants us to stay and makes it difficult to get the visas.' Again he makes the same gesture above the steering wheel with his free hand, as if something is beyond his reach.

'Why would the Church do that?' Martin asks, while Steve and I listen.

'Because they want some of the Christians to stay in Jerusalem. Everybody else wants us out. I grew up in a Christian part of Jerusalem, but now I have moved my family to Bethany.' He points toward Bethany and like a child I turn in that direction, before looking back at him. 'Every day I have to jump over the wall to take my son to a Catholic school.'

Old history, old loyalties. A part of me is impressed that someone would hold on to his religion and tradition so closely. It seems that in Jerusalem everybody does it—at any price. The Orthodox Jewish population does it. So do the Muslim Palestinians. And even the remaining Palestinian Christians. The whole city is caught in ancient, if destructive, loyalties that the rest of the world has more or less forgotten. As destructive as these loyalties are on all sides, there is a certain sense of a greater destiny present, as if people of all religious persuasions know they are a part of some cosmic warp, some ongoing debate. The city has been trapped in that warp since its beginnings. Everyone we have met has the sense there will be no way out of it until the great drama plays itself out. A grand, mad design where historical loyalties are as important now as they were fifteen hundred years ago. I have a feeling that if I ask, 'It's a medieval struggle—isn't it high time to leave the battlefield?' the answer will involve shrugged shoulders along with the reply, 'What's fifteen hundred years? It's older than that and we are all caught up in it anyway.' Indeed, what is the point? Even if you want to run, there are institutions that will prevent you from doing so, institutions that have been created ages before you.

Bethlehem looks more like a compound for prisoners than a famous historical town where pilgrims have been coming for two thousand years. It is walled-off like an open-air prison. The wall runs across the town to protect Rachel's burial place. For a foreigner it is impossible to distinguish between the propaganda of the warring parties—especially when they have been fighting for centuries. The story Charlie tells us is that the wall has been built to make it impossible for the Muslims to visit it. He isn't clear as to why. I know very little of Rachel except that she was a biblical matriarch mentioned in Genesis (29:35), the beloved wife of Jacob. It is a long and magnificent story of love and of the beginnings of Israel. Even before reading Genesis I enjoyed the fictionalised version of the story in Thomas Mann's *Joseph and His Brothers*. According to Mann's version, Jacob met Rachel when he was escaping his brother Esau's wrath. Rachel's father asked Jacob to work for him for seven years before he could marry her. After seven years, Rachel's father then tricked Jacob into marrying Rachel's sister instead. As a consequence, Jacob was forced to work an additional seven years before he was permitted to marry Rachel. And this is only the beginning of the story; I'm not going to elaborate here. Suffice to say that Rachel was an important (and romantic) biblical woman closely connected to the origins of the nation of Israel.

It is December and the weather in Bethlehem is much colder than in Jerusalem. We walk through the town, shocked by its poverty. The people look resigned. They have the familiar air of people who have learned to accept their fate because they don't see any hope or alternative for improvement in their lives.

We are completely in Charlie's hands, as he has also organised a tour guide, Bassim, for us. Bassim is a knowledgeable young man who takes us around the basilica built by Empress Helena. The only artefact from Helena's time is the mosaic on the floor. The rest was apparently added by a Byzantine emperor, Justinian. Even the basilica shows all the religious divisions of the land—the old reminders of early Christian sectarian wars. The basilica is divided into Greek and Russian Orthodox, and Catholic sections. The Catholic part is the most recent and appears to be a modern church with little feeling for the history happening below. The most moving thing for us is the little staircase which leads to the natural grotto where Yeshua was born. Finally, something personal from his life, his very beginning as a human being.

I am trying to connect with the place, but with little success. The grotto is wonderful, but it is also a tourist attraction for Christian pilgrims. As I try very hard to return to my Catholic roots by praying on my knees in front of the manger, I am interrupted by a couple of German tourists in their fifties who decide to loudly exchange comments on the spot with an African family of four.

'Here I am', I think, 'making one last effort to be a good Catholic girl (which doesn't happen very often), kneeling in front of the manger, swearing in my mind at the loud tourists. How Christian!' I double my efforts when the African family sticks their Fanta bottle into the manger, right in front of my nose, so the bottle will be blessed. I give up praying to Fanta and stand up.

'Ready to move on?' Martin asks in a matter-of-fact fashion.

'Yeah!'

All right—so I have failed to connect to the manger. There is no spiritual connection whatsoever for me; it is just an interesting place, that's all. But no connection, no spiritual revelation, no sense of Yeshua and his parents. Nothing.

The only familiar things for me are the drawings of Sts Jerome and Paula on the wall. I recognise the faint paintings immediately. They are classic symbols of Jerome. The first one I see depicts the old tale about him pulling a thorn from a lion's foot. I suddenly get excited and remember all I have learned about him and Paula: the readings I so passionately devoured in the Pontifical Library at the University of Toronto. The paintings retell the familiar story for me again: Jerome and the lion in the desert; Jerome going to Bethlehem with Paula; Jerome translating the Bible into Latin; Jerome learning Hebrew to study the Old Testament. Born in 331 CE in Dalmatia to a wealthy family, Jerome was probably of Greek descent. Educated in Rome, he decided to become a great Christian man (the Pope, preferably).

It feels like I am meeting an old friend, or perhaps a younger version of myself, hungry for knowledge, searching for the truth with great enthusiasm and then with the same zeal deconstructing the teachings and the people who pronounced them. It is almost as if I wanted to punish them for their shortcomings, which, I later learned, were also mine.

As with many other living or dead men with whom I was involved in my life, I developed a very personal relationship with Jerome. I observed him minutely—not because I believed he was a great example to follow, but because I wanted to decipher him. He was a charismatic, brilliant, difficult man. He also was a very deeply passionate and sexual man. I had a weakness for men like him, even if they had been dead for sixteen hundred years. I had an even greater weakness for them when they were alive. Fortunately for me, Jerome had been dead a very long time. What was it that fascinated me about Jerome? I didn't think much of his sainthood, but I definitely considered him an interesting man. He was an ambitious, brilliant, fiery man who struggled with his sexuality all his life. In one of his letters to a friend, he complained that women brought lust into a man's life and made him miserable. If they dressed to reveal their beauty they tortured men and brought evil, lustful thoughts and action. But if women covered themselves to hide their charms, they weren't doing a good service to men either, as they only left to men's imaginations what was hidden under their modest dresses. I thought I really understood him then. I understood his passionate whining as coming from a repressed sexuality. It was very sad, I thought, that men like that have shaped our belief about our bodies and sexuality. If sexuality was viewed as evil, how could we possibly feel comfortable in our bodies?

I loved one letter especially: '*Although my only companions were scorpions and wild beasts, time and again I mingled with the dances of girls. My face was pallid with fasting and my body chill, but my mind was throbbing with desires; my flesh was as good as dead, but the flames of lust raged in it.*'

Jerome climbed the Roman political ladder and became secretary to the Pope. When the Pope died, Jerome was bitterly disappointed that he wasn't elected his successor. He gathered his following of Roman ladies and set out for the Holy Land to set up convents in Bethlehem. His closest companion was an aristocratic Roman woman, Paula; I was especially annoyed about the role Jerome played in her daughter's life, Blesilla. At the moment when I thought I had deciphered him and could let go of my fascination with him, I wrote a story of an imaginary meeting with him in the Pontifical Library.

> Jerome waited for me between the last two rows of shelves. It was obvious he was a Roman and was on his way somewhere. He was on a ship going south, going east, going away from Rome. Enormous, fiery waves were attacking his ship. The Saints were angry, but he was going to overcome all obstacles and injustices. He

was a servant of the true God. I was ready to measure his anger against mine.

'Where are you going?' I asked him irreverently.

He gave me an annoyed look and said gloomily, 'As if you care'.

Well, I wasn't the only one in a foul mood.

'Tell me anyway.'

'I am going away from Rome, this deceitful mistress of the world. I am leaving her for the Holy Land. I worked hard for her. I was Jerome, secretary to the Pope, but Rome did not reward me for my work. I translated the Holy Scriptures and converted a multitude of Roman ladies with their pink and youthful flesh which now belongs to God alone and will never sin carnally with men. Yet when it came to elect a new Holy Father, Rome overlooked me. I am leaving her.'

'You talk of Rome as if she were a woman.'

'Ah, because she is. She is! A sinful, carnal woman who only waits for a holy man so she can seduce him, drag him down to the fires of hell. I knew many of them. The Roman ladies. All beautiful, all victims of their young flesh and carnal desires. I knew all of them. I spoke to them. I converted them. I . . .'

'I?'

'Never mind.'

'Loved them? Hated them?'

But he didn't hear me, suddenly lost in his own thoughts. Memories, perhaps.

Then, out of the blue, just as his ship was fighting the storms at their most dangerous, he whispered, 'There was one. Her name was Blesilla. They called her the beauty of Rome. So young, so delightful. So sinful. Married at an early age to control her ungodly desires, she shamelessly loved her husband. She did not complain about her marital duties as respectful women should. She enjoyed them! She never covered up her body, but instead dressed to show its sinful beauty, bringing desires to all the men of Rome. Young boys, married men, holy men. Holy men.

'She was the daughter of a Roman lady who became my disciple and my friend. But she was so unlike her mother. She laughed at her mother and sisters as they read Hebrew with me. She laughed as on my orders they flagellated and tormented their bodies so they would not bring unheavenly thoughts to men's minds. She even told them to banish me from their household and abandon the eccentricities of the aging man. I was fifty then.

'I told her a woman's flesh is sinful. If she covers her arms with a shawl, she leaves the rest to a man's imagination. He will have to think what soft and delicious flesh, what pink, young skin is hidden behind the material, and in thinking about it, he will not think of God.'

'Should she uncover her arms then?' I asked.

'That would be even worse. To expose her sinful body for the enjoyment of men who would eat her with their eyes, if not'—the Saint lifted up his eyes to Heaven—'with their very tongues and mouths. They would lick her in their minds and the most sinful ones would come to her, deceive her with earthly pleasures, do all of these things to her with their physical bodies, bringing her and themselves to eternal damnation.'

Wow! I needed a moment to catch my breath. That bad! 'And what did she say?'

'At first she laughed, but the wrath of God came upon her. Her husband died from the fever that comes seasonally to Rome. And by the wise judgment of God, her husband was not spared so she could learn the lesson and change her incorrigible behaviour.

'I found her once sitting in the courtyard of her mother's mansion. I could feel she was in a penitential mood, broken by her husband's death. I knew that the fruit was ripe and she, with the provocation of her young body and the stubbornness of her soul, was finally delivered to me. To my hands. I sat by her side and saw tears in her beautiful eyes—eyes that used to bring so many men to desperation. I took her by her hand (small and delicate like the petal of a flower) and talked to her about the suffering of our God. For the first time she listened. I saw that her face was devoured by fever. Her face was aflame from my words.'

'Maybe she was sick?' I interrupted.

'Yes, she was sick!' the Saint exploded impatiently. 'That is beside the point. She was listening. For the first time I could sit by her, I could touch her hand, I could see her beauty—and she listened. She did not laugh at me. She listened. With tears in her lovely eyes, trembling with desire for God as I caressed her hand. That evening I thanked God for his grace and wisdom'.

I felt nauseous and I don't think it was because the Saint's ship was moving so fast. I think I just wanted to vomit.

'She felt worse on the following day.'

'That doesn't surprise me', I said, but the Saint ignored me.

'She was so sick with fever she had to stay in bed. I visited her regularly and spoke to her about the eternal fires of hell that awaited her if she didn't recover. She listened, her forehead covered in sweat. She listened. I administered penitence for her and told her that if she fasted, if she flagellated her sinful body, God would forgive her trespasses and save her from damnation. She listened. She refused all food. She allowed me to put a coarse, dirty cloth on her body, once so used to the finest fabrics. She suffered like the martyrs. I told her that there was hope for her.'

The Saint paused in holy contemplation, then continued. 'Within two weeks she died. I know she went to heaven. Paula, her mother, knows it too. Paula thanked me for saving her daughter for God. But Rome—worldly, sinful Rome—was outraged with me, outraged with Paula. They called her a bad mother and a mad woman. They called me a mad ascetic, a dangerous and extreme man. I had to leave. That is why I am on my way to the Holy Land. I will start houses for women and bring them back to the path of virtue, just as I brought beautiful Blesilla back to God'.

'Nunneries?'

'Yes, houses of God.'

I left the Saint in the library, feeling some relief at knowing that his misery was greater than mine. But there was no light. He was left in his darkness. I was stuck with my doubts.

I am troubled by my experience in the manger. Am I, like many other Catholics, so removed from the reality of Yeshua's life that I connect better with the Saints, even those I don't like? In some profound and bizarre way I feel connected to them, as if they are difficult childhood cousins I can't stand. Why do I know so much more about Jerome and Paula than what happened to me in the manger? Naturally, I know all the cute stories about Yeshua's birth that we were told as children, but even they are covered with layers of legend and church dogma. They are either naively childlike or simply implausible—like the virgin birth. Too many layers of interference and interpretation. I feel that I can't cross the sea of history between us.

Back on the street Steve buys me a milky drink from an old street peddler. The peddler produces the drink like a magician from a tall silver dish which he carries on his cart. It is warm and sweet, with walnuts and raisins—one positive, human experience from Bethlehem. We are tourists, but the peddler—a kind, sadly smiling man—charges us almost nothing for the drink. I know I will love this memory of Bethlehem.

Meanwhile, Bassim takes Martin to a souvenir shop. We see Martin there buying figurines of 'Mary, Joseph and the baby Jesus' for his grandchildren, even though he is aware his son doesn't want them to be brought up in any religious way. Another old man—the owner of the store, or perhaps the maker of the nativity figurines—brings some tea for us.

'I'll just tell them the story from a human perspective', Martin says, playing with the figurines as if disputing the wisdom of buying them at all.

I have mixed feelings about the store. It reminds me of the many *devotionalia* shops I saw in Poland. On the one hand, I can't help but feel the respect instilled in me since childhood for all religious matters. On the other hand, I feel how kitschy it all is. The perfume of Mary Magdalene, supposedly the ointment she poured on Yeshua's body; the wooden figurines, looking exactly as western tradition renders them; the young, virginal Mary and the old Joseph. I know that Joseph's old age was always overemphasised to make the story of the immaculate conception more credible. Good old Joseph would never do it with young Mary, right?

I regret the poverty of the people in Bethlehem, but I don't like the pressure to 'support the poor Christians of Bethlehem' as Charlie puts it. I have too many problems with the story and how it was created in the collective imagination. I am fond of my childhood memories of family Christmas' with my nana and mum cooking in the kitchen for Christmas Eve, but I am also profoundly sick and tired of it. I don't care about being Christian in any conventional sense. I don't care for kitschy sentimental souvenirs that support the story. I don't like the fact that being in the store itself is some kind of forced declaration of faith—a faith conflicting with other faiths which are equally valid. I feel that by bringing us here, Charlie is forcing me to make the same declaration he made when he stopped his taxi on the Mount of Olives and offered to take us to Bethlehem. I don't want to make that declaration, as I feel it is old, harmful and outdated.

Why can't we say to each other that we are all children of God? Great beings of all religious persuasions walked that magnificent land; why don't we honour that? People should stop obsessing about minute attachments and about the different ways they worship because God *manifests* in each person's life in individual ways. Why do we have to say: I am a Jew, I am a Christian, I am a Muslim?

I want to have a sense of who Yeshua was as a man—perhaps I have found it somehow in the face of the sad old Palestinian street peddler. But I have not found it in the basilica and I have not found it in the souvenir shop.

'A shop of made-up stories', I think as I pay for the ointment of Mary Magdalene with a picture of a blond woman on the bottle.

It is raining in Jerusalem when Charlie drops us by St Stephen's Gate. It is our first cold, rainy day in the city.

We walk through the nearly empty Armenian quarter. I marvel again at the medieval nature of the city. In other cities, things change, lose their significance—life moves on. Not in Jerusalem. If something was important once, even for a brief moment, it will stay important forever. I marvel at the grandiose feel of everything here. I marvel at the invincibility of history and passions, and I can't help but smile and feel happy. Why? Hasn't this caused all the problems? All the outdated loyalties and histories? The same part of me that made me study medieval history and philosophy delights in the city and its history. In a world where everything is temporary and lasts about five seconds, all here is eternal. It is a dangerous eternity, full of unresolved anger and misunderstandings, but it is eternity nonetheless.

Slowly we make our way to the Damascus Gate, besieged by tiny Palestinian shops selling cheap perfume, underwear, spices, clocks and who-knows-what. Martin and I go to the Internet cafe. Steve heads off to an archaeological store looking for artefacts from Yeshua's times.

It is raining even more when I leave the Internet cafe: an annoying, persistent drizzle. A perfect mirror of how I feel about myself that day. I join Steve in the archaeological store and help him choose an antique oil lamp.

'You can treat yourself sometimes, you know', I say, encouraging him to buy the lamp. It looks like a small vessel of light. I imagine people throughout history in Jerusalem, leaning over the light, writing, reading, trying to convey something that cannot be captured well enough with words. Words. What a tool, yet how insufficient they are sometimes. But words are often all we have. 'A little human touch', I say and brush against his shoulder, but he moves away.

Martin comes out of the Internet cafe and joins us. The three of us walk towards the bus station near the Damascus Gate. The rain intensifies and we have no choice but to catch a taxi to the hotel. Steve goes back to his room while Martin and I share a hot pot of tea in the restaurant downstairs. I think of the events of the day, wondering what it all means. I feel sad and emotionally drained.

I say to Martin, 'I'm tired of the turbulence and intensity of my emotions. I'd like to see the design of life through God's eyes. How does God see it? Beauty in suffering? Peace in drama?'

Martin just sits there quietly next to me, and touches my hand in a fatherly gesture, 'You will find peace', he says and somehow this strengthens me enough to go back to my room and write in my journal.

Hours later, in my room, I lie down on my bed with my pen and journal next to me. Just before sunrise I feel I am floating above Jerusalem in the strange ecstasy of those who have nothing to lose. The city is beautifully lit. I talk to the city as one talks to a lover one has known for only a brief time: 'In my life I've had no security, only powerful desires, a fiery soul, curious mind and passionate relationships with men and God. My way of making sense of it all has always been with writing. I don't know where you'll take me from this moment on, but you've certainly made sure I learn to trust you, as I have nothing else. I have no illusions. At the moment I have no influence on my life either. And a powerful desire has brought me here—a fire from my soul, a desire I don't understand which has overwhelmed me completely. Perhaps it's about making peace with Yeshua, making friends with the most mysterious of divine beings? I've walked where he walked. I've visited places where he was born and suffered. I've connected to his suffering in the olive grove on the Mount of Olives. I'm not repulsed by his suffering anymore. We can be friends now.' I have no clue what this means.

THE HOUSE

The Holy Land. 'Holy' in the way the early Saints were holy—seriously eccentric, manic and, at times, sublime.

This is the land which inspired all the ecstatics of Judaism, Christianity and Islam.

The land of rebellious rabbis. Yeshua was one of them.

The land of St Anthony, who lived in the desert, doing his best to resist the temptation of a beautiful seductress.

The land of Simeon Stylites, who spent his life standing on a tall column and meditating.

The rationale of their actions escapes me, but I love their holy madness. How different were their actions from the crazy things any lover does for a beloved? Standing at the window hoping for a glance of him? Falling for a beauty who can only bring pain in return? When I read the accounts of those charismatic and eccentric Saints, those extreme Saints, I think of crimes of passion.

Why am I thinking these things? As much as I don't want to be caught up in the madness, I can't help but think of the religious tradition in which I was brought up. The fact that I was completely unhappy with this tradition and abandoned it doesn't matter here. I am still consumed by the mental references to this tradition which I thought I had forgotten a long time ago.

As if this personal preoccupation with the past is not enough, we are being driven to Nazareth by Charlie's friend. The same Charlie who took us to Bethlehem and organised a Palestinian-Christian tour guide. Now a friend of his is taking us to Nazareth. 'This land', I catch myself thinking, 'is like some religious mafia. Once you say "yes" you are sucked in with no way out'. I breathe out and release some tension in my chest. *I'm not really a part of that, I won't allow myself to be a part of that.*

The drive to Nazareth takes two hours and fifteen minutes. Nazareth is a picturesque, hilly town. There is a soft charm about the place: *Christmas in Nazareth.* The driver leaves us at the door of the Convent of the Sisters of Nazareth, where we are to stay. Ala'a, the manager of the place, is a young French-speaking man who knows Steve well from his previous trips here. He shows us our rooms, one per person, and invites us for a meal in a dining room the sisters have organised for 'pilgrims'. I like this. The convent doesn't look much different from what I imagined when I first heard of it back in Steve's apartment in Richmond. But I haven't anticipated the new construction, the new guests' quarters. I had hoped we would live in the convent and eat with the nuns. In reality, they live separate lives from their guests, even if they are polite and welcoming.

I like being called a pilgrim. A pilgrim is a seeker on a sublime mission, searching for something higher than the concerns which determine our lives on a daily basis. I think of a pilgrim as someone who, by choice, wants to live on the edge and seek answers to questions that only a few dare to ask. I made this choice long ago. I was born knowing I would become this—a pilgrim, someone who wants to know and experience the truth and the search for truth. Truth can have many faces, but for me it has always been a combination of knowledge, experience and love. I have seen people I love, my friends and family, struggling with choices, asking themselves who they are, asking themselves about the purpose of life. As a pilgrim I have always had a clear purpose, even if I have often screamed, had tantrums and rebelled against it. In some perverse way, all is perfect at this moment as we are shown our rooms in the guest house of the Sisters of Nazareth.

I have nothing. I feel like nothing. 'I am stripped of everything', I tell Steve as we walk to the small dining room downstairs. There is nothing to support me in ordinary terms: no job, no relationship, no place to live upon my return to Melbourne, no status.

And yet? And yet I am here, feeling the same passion I have always felt in my life whenever I moved in the right direction. That same unshakable, inner conviction that can't be explained to anyone, because in rational terms it makes absolutely no sense. In my worst moments I imagine my friends and family shaking their heads and saying, 'Poor Joanna'. And make no mistake, I am usually the first one to feel sorry for myself and to wave my fist at the heavens when things don't go my way.

I wake up in the morning, at the moment of greatest pain and self-doubt, full of fear and angst, and yet I feel an indescribable bliss coming from a mysterious part of me—a bliss so convincing that I know I am in the right place at the right time, doing the right thing, even if it doesn't make any sense to my frustrated, scared mind.

The Holy Land still attracts strange clientele, and from what I can see not much has changed since Simon the Stylite. (Not that we are 'normal' by any standards, mind you.) That same evening a lost Frenchman called Jonathan shows up at the gates, claiming he has been robbed in Tiberias, and that his passport and wallet have been stolen. He has no money, no ID, no suitcase.

The sisters have doubts about his story, but they let him in and allow him to sleep in a small reading room by the foyer. The French consulate will open after the holidays, so his situation will be sorted out one way or another. Sister Margherita tells Steve that every Christmas they find someone like that at the gates—as if Christmas is a special call for lost souls. I sit on the bench in the courtyard as Martin hurries out to his room to get Jonathan some toiletries.

'Do you think his story is true?' I hear an older French woman asking. I smile. *Does it matter?*

Many years ago, in Paris, I knocked on the door of a convent run by a Polish nun, Sister Maria, to ask for shelter. It was before Christmas, I was nineteen, in Paris, and in need of refuge. I had just left Eastern Europe forever, but I didn't know it then. I thought I had come to Paris for Christmas as a lucky fluke—not a bad thing for a Polish girl caught behind the communist wall which had separated her from her dreams of experiencing the wider world, dreams of Paris and its artistic past and promise. I wanted to breathe the air Modigliani had breathed. I wanted to sit in the cafe where Beauvoir and Sartre wrote and drank their cafés au lait. I wanted to hang out at the bookstore where Hemingway borrowed books from Sylvia Beach. I wanted it all—and more. I wanted a perfect escape from the limitations of Eastern Europe and the communist system. And most of all, I wanted to discover myself, to fulfil my potential as a woman, as a writer, as a decadent libertine who believed that dreams come true through the sheer power of desire.

My mother's boyfriend worked in Paris as a hired hand at some construction site and he said I could stay with him throughout my two-week holiday. He lived in a tiny mansard right under the rooftop. 'How Parisian!' I thought. My girlfriend Jola, from my philosophy course at the university, had organised a legal invitation for me from a French family—a document necessary for Polish police to issue a passport and for the French Embassy to issue me with a visa. I had ten borrowed dollars in my pocket—the amount of money that was allowed to be taken out of Poland. So there I was, with my dream fulfilled, in Paris. Two days before Christmas. Some people might have said I was in Paris, but I knew I was in heaven. I had never seen anything so beautiful. The writers who lived there were my Saints. The artists who painted there were my angels. But even heaven has its dark side. Soon after my arrival, my mother's boyfriend began introducing me to his friends as his girlfriend. In the evening he insisted we sleep in the one bed. A huge screaming battle followed. I slammed the door and left. Jola told me about Sister Maria, a Polish nun who ran a convent on the outskirts of Paris, and within hours I was at her door asking for help on Christmas Eve. So, yes, I was inclined to believe Jonathan's story.

The sisters invite us to dinner with the other guests. The dining room is newly built, clean and has a rustic look with perfectly ironed and starched red-and-white-checked linen tablecloths—something you might expect when visiting your European nana's country house. We are served *arak* (an alcoholic drink with aniseed) to start, which I think is very civilised, especially for a convent, then receive a soup with home-made white bread and butter. We can't get enough of the bread and ask for another portion before we learn there is also a main course: chicken and vegies. In the dining room are a few pilgrims, two older French couples, one young Japanese man busily hiding behind the book he is reading, and Bernard. Bernard is a tall, sturdily built, dramatic man in his late fifties. He looks like an excellent specimen of health, vitality and joviality. From the moment we enter the dining room and sit at our table he watches us expectantly, hoping to catch our attention. I smile at him and ask, '*Vous êtes Français?*'

'*Mais oui!*' he responds enthusiastically, and immediately joins us at our table.

He introduces himself and before I have a chance to respond he manages to tell us the story of his life and the reason why he is in Nazareth this Christmas. He is writing a book on Charles de Foucault.

'Have you heard of him *Mademoiselle?*' he asks. '*Non? Ah bon*, he was a Trappist monk who lived in the Holy Land, *et voil`a!* Here is the book I am writing about him.'

'Oh', I say innocently. 'I can see beautiful illustrations but no writing.'

'Ah! *Pas de problem!* I started the illustrations about the places he visited and now I will do the rest of the research on him here.'

'I see. Good idea!' I laugh, enjoying his audacity.

'And what's your name *Mademoiselle?*' he finally asks me.

'Joanna', I say, pointing at myself, then at the others, 'and Steve and Martin.'

'Ah! Pleasure to meet you,' Bernard pours more of his joviality on us.

He then shows us a children's book about an old oak tree that used to 'live' on his property in France and has recently been cut down. At the word *cut*, Bernard re-enacts the cutting of the tree for us with what appears to be an electric saw.

'That's terrible!' I exclaim, caught like a child in his dramatic narration.

'Why!?' Even always-cool Steve is temporarily disturbed.

'The tree was terribly old and sick', Bernard says tragically. 'It would have fallen on the house in a day or two if we had not cut it.' This time he enacts the imaginary, cutting his own throat.

'Ah! That's okay then,' I say. Steve and I are relieved, while Martin has a great time, watching us with amusement.

'I must go now. I will be joining the French group here on the trip to Tiberias. Every tour group needs a troublemaker, you see.' Bernard says, 'But before I go away I want to admire the view'.

'The view?'

'*Mais oui*. Joanna from the right side, Joanna from the left side. Very nice view from all sides.'

'It's a scary thing', Martin sums up philosophically. 'We're in the Holy Land and we're a prime attraction for Frenchmen.'

When Steve first visited Nazareth, the place was deserted because it was 2000, the year of the *Intifada*. When he stepped out of the bus near the Christian Basilica, all the hotels were closed. There he was in Nazareth, knocking on the doors of hotels without any luck. At one of the places, a man stuck his head out of the third floor window and yelled, 'What do you want?'

'I'm after a bed', he yelled back.

'I can't help you.'

'Any idea who *can* help?'

'Try the Sisters of Nazareth.'

The Sisters of Nazareth did have a room and that's where he stayed for a week. He was the only guest.

His intention was to approximate the location of Yeshua's house in old Nazareth. From the descriptions in *The Urantia Book*, he guessed roughly where the house might be. The descriptions were quite detailed. They gave three points of reference: the top of the hill, the road to Cana, and the direction from Mary's well. Steve did some basic triangulations to help determine the location. On his first morning in Nazareth he went down to breakfast with the sisters. He sat at a table overlooking purple bougainvillea flowers in the courtyard and unfolded his map. His plan was to walk around the area where Yeshua had walked. He was gathering an idea of the location of the well on the map and some other details of the landscape in the area. The sisters became curious and asked him about the lines drawn on his map.

'Oh, I just want to get the feel of the place, and I think Jesus grew up somewhere around here', he said, preoccupied.

He got up from his table, took his camera, map and compass, and headed off around Nazareth, taking measurements and more readings. As he walked around the hilly area near the convent he thought, 'That's interesting. Where I'm staying is quite close to the house'. He took measurements for most of the day, stopping only for lunch at a kebab place on the main street.

The next morning Sister Margherita came up to him and said, 'You are not the normal type of tourist we usually get here'.

'I'm not, am I?' he laughed in that self-deprecating way she had noticed about Australian tourists. 'I just have a deep interest in it.'

She looked at him intently and said, 'You might be interested in an archaeological site, under the church here. Would you like to see it?'

Steve had planned to continue with his measurements for the house of Joseph where the young Jesus had lived, but he consented. After all, he had plenty of time and he could afford some kindness to the sister.

They walked out to the courtyard. Sister Margherita opened up the steel gates to the excavations and they walked downstairs along marble steps leading underground. She turned the lights on. The excavations continued all the way down. As they descended he looked up and saw a Byzantine copula above, which was about a thousand years old. They kept walking deeper into the excavations until they came to a well half filled with water. To their left, carved out of the rock, were two thousand-year-old water basins for washing.

But the best was yet to come. Sister Margherita said, 'Look at this'. They walked around the corner and stepped into what was a first-century home. Steve was staggered because it had two rooms and the plan matched the descriptions in *The Urantia Book* perfectly. When Joseph and Mary married they had had a house with a single room, but later on Joseph had built a second room which was used as a workshop.

'Coincidences happen', he thought.

On the floor of the house lay Roman paving stones which had been put down a little bit later to protect the floor from too many visitors. Two flights of stairs had also been added afterwards: another sign that lots of people visited the place. Sister Margherita allowed Steve to absorb what he saw in silence without seeking a response. She stood there like a silent guide. When she thought he had seen enough she led him back upstairs, and he returned to the hills to make more measurements and continue his private experience of the young Yeshua. He spent another day walking, searching and making careful measurements. That night, at about two in the morning, he woke up in his bed sweating, 'This is it! This is his house. I'm sleeping on top of it'. He had been searching for the house all around where it was actually located! As if the possibility of it was already there waiting to be named, too much to digest for the rational mind.

Steve got up from his bed, went to his suitcase and carefully opened *The Urantia Book*. 'What the hell', he thought. 'I'll check if the house under the convent matches the descriptions from *The Urantia Book*.' He read aloud from the book: 'The home of Jesus was not far from the hill in the northerly part of Nazareth, some distance from the village spring, which was in the eastern section of the town. Jesus' family dwelt in the outskirts of the city . . .'

Steve paused here and mumbled something to himself, skipped some lines, then continued: 'Here Jesus made frequent trips up to the top of this nearby highland, the highest of all the hills of southern Galilee save for the Mount Tabor range to the east and the hill of Nain, which was about the same height . . . Their home was located a little to the south and east of the southern promontory of this hill and about midway between the base of this elevation and the road leading out of Nazareth toward Cana'.

After a restless night he went to the breakfast room early, anxiously waiting for the sisters.

117

'Do you realise what you have here?' he yelled in excitement when they came down with coffee. But the sisters were quiet. He drank his coffee, but couldn't eat anything. He couldn't understand the sisters' lack of response. So he got up, went back to the hills behind the convent and took more measurements. He originally thought a church on the top of the hill was the place from where he needed to measure. But it wasn't. At the very top of the hill was a water reservoir, and when he took measurements from there they all pointed to the excavation Sister Margherita had shown him.

Steve went to check his readings against this information. His original estimates had the house located between streets 6173 and 6156; the convent was situated only 150 metres to the east. So that morning he went again to confirm his measurements. On the way to the top of the hill he found a small path along an old water reservoir close to the hill's peak between the Church of the Adolescent Jesus and the Mosque of Nabi Saen. This was the perfect place for a reservoir, as the water would have maximum fall from this highest point. The spot was about 150 metres east of the site where Steve had originally taken the measurements. His new readings indicated that the house was right under the convent, which also happened to be halfway between the promontory and the road to Cana, now called Paulus VI.

Steve went back to the sisters, telling them that, according to his measurements, this was the house.

They were very cautious. 'Maybe', they replied.

He was suspicious of their lukewarm response and decided to do some research on the house. The Franciscans from St. Joseph's Church across the street from the sisters claimed Joseph's workshop was in the cavern under their church, so perhaps the sisters didn't want to rock the boat? But the sisters were not completely disinterested or unwilling to name the excavations under their convent. As Steve was finishing his breakfast, Sister Margherita, who was sitting across the table, told him in a conspiratorial tone more about the history of the site. The site had always been known as the 'home of the Saint', she told him, even when there had been no visible home on the site. When the sisters had made an offer on the land about one hundred and fifty years previously, the owners had remarked, 'Be careful. This is the home of the Saint'. Yet there was nothing there. The site was discovered only with the commencement of the convent's construction.

'There was so much activity around this site for so long— there has to be a reason for it', Sister Margherita said.

'What sort of activity?'

'Some priest appears to be buried next to the home. Underneath the home, someone has constructed a tomb with a rolling-door closure. Also, a crusader's spurs were discovered there. The crusader had come from France to this place and hung up his spurs on the wall of the house. This kind of thing was done only in holy places. So you see how much attention this place has had. It's extraordinary, isn't it?'

Another sister called out to her in French. Sister Margherita apologised for talking too much and left.

But that was more than enough for Steve by then. He wanted to know more about the site. Sister Margherita gave him the key so he could revisit the excavated house under the convent, where this time he took pictures. He breathed more deeply as he went down there by himself.

'It's the house where Jesus grew up', he kept thinking. He entered the first room, which was much more modest and smaller than the second room, which had been built later. According to what he had read about the house, it all made sense. Joseph, Yeshua's father, had been poor at that time and they had built the additional room when things picked up a little. In the first room, Steve sat at the stone slab which had once served as a table. He sat cross-legged at the table where Yeshua had eaten his meals. For a while he couldn't move—out of emotion, out of elation.

Steve's most moving discovery in the house was a game board chiselled in stone, about 73 centimetres square and 23 centimetres deep. He later learned from a specialist on games that it was one of the most popular ancient games, known as Nine Men's Morris—a combination of checkers and tic-tac-toe. Imagine young Jesus playing a game with his brothers and sisters. This was what Steve had always wanted: to meet Yeshua as a person and not as some enigmatic religious figure. Yeshua, the man and the son. That was enough for Steve to change his travel itinerary. Instead of going to Lebanon as planned, he stayed in Israel and continued looking for an archaeological study that had been done on the site by a Father Senes around seventy years earlier.

The nuns had told Steve about Father Senes. They were in no hurry to share information about the excavations; the disclosures trickled in every morning, over breakfast. He listened, then took notes later in his room. The trip to Lebanon was definitely out of the question now. Instead, he went to the École Biblique and the Rockefeller Library in Jerusalem to look for documentation on excavations conducted under the convent in the past. His curiosity was heightened when he found cards in the filing systems about archaeological studies under the convent, but when he went looking for the documents they weren't there. The strange disappearance of documents from such venerable institutions only strengthened his resolve to unravel the mystery. The experiences from Nazareth sparked a journey to various places in search of a set of the archaeological notes made by Father Senes.

It was important to the sisters, he thought, to have the documentation—for historical value, if nothing else. Still, Steve sometimes asked himself, 'Why do I bother? All this expense. Am I mad?' The more he thought about it, the more he realised that his primary concern was to gather professional archaeological information and cultural information and, most of all, to preserve the site. Not to inform the world about it necessarily, but to preserve it. An announcement was tempting, but that decision belonged to the sisters. He felt he would be betraying their confidence, even if they had never asked for secrecy. But the situation was touchy when it concerned an issue of this kind. *The house of Joseph—where Yeshua grew up.* Imagine that. During his subsequent visits, Steve took his camera gear and photographed every brick, every stone of the building.

Once he felt there was a good chance it was Yeshua's childhood home, he allowed the news to wash over him. For Steve, Nazareth was about family, about growing up. Yeshua had been happy there; he had lived a normal life. Steve wanted to experience that part of Yeshua's life. And that part of himself. Perhaps he was also looking for a happy childhood of his own and wanted to recapture it through Yeshua's life. For Steve, Nazareth was a paradigm of happy childhood, regardless of his later suffering in adulthood. Sometimes I wondered why it was so important for him. Steve pictured the young Yeshua learning to read, with his mother preparing food in the kitchen with his sisters; young Jesus taking harp lessons; learning carpentry from his father in the second room of the house, which was a workshop during the day and the second bedroom at night; young Yeshua sleeping peacefully at night with his parents and siblings. Wasn't that what images of the Holy Family had always been? This was an example every Christian, especially Catholics, had been taught. On a deeper emotional level, Steve was looking for proof of this in Nazareth.

I am more sceptical. I tend to have more realistic views on family: some family members are supportive, but many are controlling. I couldn't wait to be old enough to leave my family behind. I harboured no hard feelings—just an immense thirst for the adventure of life. For the unlimited adventure of life and freedom. Freedom! The sweetest word in the world for me during my twenties and thirties. But Steve was looking for a happy family five years after his divorce. He loved Nazareth.

And Jerusalem? He found Jerusalem more dramatic. *Too* dramatic. Nazareth represented for him the essence of what Yeshua taught: God is loving and therefore we all are God's spiritual children; we are connected, we are all brothers and sisters. For Steve, the Nazareth house was the symbolic centre of this teaching. All these ideas of belonging—belonging to the universe, being loved, of connecting with other people regardless of their culture or religion—were about being a part of one spiritual family. With all humankind. It took Steve a long time to digest this. He didn't try to convince anyone that this could be *the home*. To most people this might be no more than a wonderful example of a first-century home, but for him it became a great personal journey.

Steve found out that a Jesuit priest trained as an archaeologist had spent some time on the site. His name was Father Silvio. The sisters told Steve that Father Silvio worked in Rome, but also had an apartment in Amsterdam. Since Steve couldn't find any of Father Senes' notes in the Jerusalem libraries, he decided he would visit Father Silvio and ask him if he knew anything about them. But Steve let it go for two years.

A couple of years later Steve was in Paris at a conference with a friend, Neil, and suggested they take a train to Amsterdam to look for Father Silvio. Steve had Father Silvio's phone number and called him several times from Paris, but never got a reply. One time Father Silvio's secretary, Dominique, answered but she gave no definite indication that they might meet. Steve and Neil discussed the pros and cons of the matter in a cafe in Marais in Paris. Steve finished his *crème brûlée* and said to Neil, 'Why don't we just go?'

Steve usually wrote a list with two columns—'for' and 'against'—for every significant decision in his life. Based on the outcome of this calculation, he made his decisions. Except . . . he never actually acted on the cold calculations, the rational decisions. There was always something to interfere with his precise calculations. Some magnificent piece of information. Some mystery that couldn't be treated by the scalpel of the mind, but had to be touched with the softest of touches, with intuition and imagination. At that particular moment he said with definite certainty, 'The Flow wants us to go there'.

'But we've just weighed up all the pros and cons', Neil argued, stunned by the sudden turn. 'We'd already decided it didn't make sense to go—it costs money and will probably lead nowhere. And now you just finish your dessert and say, "Why don't we go?" and "The Flow wants us to go there". What's this bloody "Flow"? Is it something in your *crème brûlée*?'

Poor Neil. If 'the Flow' told Steve to go somewhere, there was no stopping him. Worse still, 'the Flow' usually spread over any unsuspecting companion who happened to be there with Steve when It announced Its decision and you were forced to follow too.

The next day they took a train from Paris to Amsterdam. They argued all the way to Amsterdam, which kept them awake and made the trip seem shorter. Once in Amsterdam, they left the main station and started looking for the street where Father Silvio lived. They had the name of the street but not the number, meaning they had to guess. At the end of the street they saw a cottage completely overgrown with creepers; Steve declared to Neil that he knew it was the place.

'How?' Neil asked.

'It feels right', Steve retorted seriously.

They knocked on the door and Dominique, the secretary, opened it. She was expecting them, she said, and showed them in. They sat down at a big oak table and waited until Father Silvio, a very focused, alert man in his late fifties, walked in.

Steve was stunned. The elusive Father Silvio, who had the key to the mystery of the house in Nazareth, was standing right in front of them. The Flow had been right again, but he thought better of rubbing it in to Neil.

After recovering from the sight of Father Silvio, Steve began to stutter like a nervous student: 'H-Hello. We bring . . . uh . . . g-greetings from the Sisters of Nazareth'.

Father Silvio looked intrigued, and a bit amused. He raised his eyebrows and smiled.

Steve cleared his throat. 'I'm looking for some of Father Senes' archaeological notes.'

Father Silvio leaned towards him and said, 'They are very rare'.

But Steve was on a mission now and regained his clarity. 'I know. I've been looking for them for two years.'

Father Silvio nodded thoughtfully, as if considering a life decision. He looked again at Steve and said, 'Wait'.

He disappeared behind the door while Steve and Neil stared at the ceiling. After about half an hour, Father Silvio came back with a huge pile of books, about eight volumes. He put the books on the tables in piles. 'The first pile', he said, 'is Father Senes' archaeological notes. The second pile is my private notes on the site; the third pile is secondary references from pilgrims who have travelled through the place'.

'Do you believe', Steve gathered the courage to ask, 'that the house under the convent is the home of Jesus?'

Steve would never forget this moment: Father Silvio simply stated in a matter-of-fact way, 'Yes'.

Later Steve asked himself if Father Silvio was even allowed to admit this, since the official home of Jesus, according to the Catholic Church, was supposed to be where the Franciscans indicated.

Suddenly Father Silvio looked exhausted. He slid the books across the table as if to say, 'I don't want to know about this. It is yours. You are welcome to copy these books'. And he left the room.

Dominique followed him out then came back to show them Father Silvio's library, complete with a photocopier. Steve looked at the two-storey-high rows of books. Dominique noticed his reaction and told him there were over fifty thousand religious texts in the library and that Father Silvio had given them permission to look over them freely. Over two hours Neil and Steve made two sets of copies of all the documents from the three piles. They worked in a trance, aware they were photocopying priceless materials that biblical archaeologists around the world would kill for. Why had Father Silvio decided to share this treasure with them and not serious academics? Maybe he wanted to let this part of his life go. Maybe he didn't want ambitious professors using it as a stepping-stone to academic fame and promotion. Who knew? Or maybe, just maybe, like everyone else who met Steve, Father Silvio trusted his integrity and, as a religious man and priest, he saw the honesty of Steve's intentions. Perhaps

Father Silvio wanted the world to know about the results of his excavations, but being a Catholic priest, couldn't announce them himself. The point was that Neil and Steve walked out onto the street, looked at the two bags of documents they carried, and said in one voice, 'Can you believe this?'

They decided Neil would take one set to Australia with him while Steve took the other set to the Sisters of Nazareth. Steve flew back to Jerusalem, hopped on the bus to Nazareth, and told the sisters he had a gift for them. They all came down to the dining room where Steve pulled out all the notes and references. The sisters started to dance down the hallway singing 'Thank you, thank you' in unison like little girls who had received a Christmas gift.

Steve faced a dilemma. After the trip to Amsterdam his conviction that this was the house of Jesus had strengthened. He didn't want to stop the investigation, and even thought of collecting DNA samples from the site to compare with the DNA from the Turin Shroud. He thought this was possible since the Roman stones had preserved the floor and everything around it. That was too much for the sisters. They sent Sister Margherita out to speak to Steve.

'Look, Steve', she said. 'It's for the best if we just don't tell anyone about this.' They weren't ready. So Steve dropped the matter.

Things are a little bit simpler for me. I want to get over the naïve story about the virgin birth, about women confirming Mary's virginity after she gave birth to Yeshua. Traditionally, the Russian and Greek Orthodox Churches believed that Joseph,

Yeshua's father, might have had children who were Yeshua's half-siblings from a previous marriage, and that Mary gave birth to Yeshua without having sexual contact with Joseph or any other man. A virgin birth. Later, the more sober Protestants believed in the virgin birth of Yeshua, but conceded that Mary subsequently had other children with Joseph. The Catholics, on the other hand, insisted that Mary was a virgin before, during, and after the birth. Perpetual virginity. The most radical source for this notion was the *Protoevangelium of James*, written about 124 CE, which initiated the idea of perpetual virginity. In it, the midwife present at Yeshua's birth confirms to Salome that she has witnessed a miracle: a virgin birth. Salome (unsurprisingly) says she won't believe it until she 'thrusts her finger' into Mary's womb to check for herself. She does, and confirms Mary's virginity.

Am I the only person who struggles to comprehend the story? I want something I can grasp, or relate to, something that will give me guidance through the maze of living. I'm not a happy little schoolgirl full of bizarre, if cute, stories about Jesus in Bethlehem, the three kings and animals talking at midnight anymore. I want to understand something of the story—to find faults with it if necessary, to straighten it up or complicate it—so that a modern person can relate to it, can benefit from the teachings, can know Yeshua. I want to know him better, beyond the mythological folk-tales, the sexual repression and the neuroses of the ascetic men who led the Church after Yeshua's physical death. Beyond the politics of the gospels, beyond the canonisation process in the fourth century which rejected some gospels because they were considered too radical, or written by women, or simply because some powerful bishop didn't like them.

I want to know *him*.

It is Christmas Eve and I decide to give in to my traditional Catholic upbringing and go to the Franciscan Church of Annunciation to celebrate. Steve and Martin have decided they will wait for me and we will find a nice place later for dinner. The church is across the street from the Sisters of Nazareth. I see a crowd of people outside the church and join the queue. At the door I am told I can't come in without a ticket.

I am stunned and ask the man at the door, 'Are you telling me I can't participate in the religious service celebrating the birth of Jesus without a ticket? I came all the way from Australia and I can't come in, right?'

'You can't come in without a ticket', he confirms gravely. 'You don't have to pay but you need a ticket.'

I do my best not to have a full-blown fit. What a good lesson for me—to make peace with tradition! The irony of the situation is beyond me. Two men who would never turn away another human being seeking peace would be Jesus and St Francis. Can you imagine Jesus asking people for a ticket to listen to him teach at a synagogue in Capernaum, or anywhere else for that matter? *My Peace I give, but first—did you buy a ticket?* I don't think so. *Oh, some fish and bread for the poor? Not without a ticket, right?* I could just imagine his apostles yelling, 'Tickets! Tickets! Jesus is in town!' Or what about Saint Francis, the outrageous son of a wealthy Florentine merchant, who stripped himself of his clothes after a wild night with his friends, and at that very moment decided to live in imitation of Christ and serve the poor? Would he ask for a ticket if someone came to celebrate Jesus' birth with him? I mumble to myself as I walk back to the Sisters of Nazareth. Ala'a, the manager, opens the gate for me. 'I couldn't get in because I didn't have a ticket!' I yell at the gate, expecting compassion. But Ala'a is in a managerial, not mystical, mood and says quietly in his French accent, 'But of course you need a ticket for a function like that'.

'Function?' I scream in horror. 'You call it a function?'

Ala'a keeps his cool. 'You can always try to negotiate with them.'

'I'm too appalled to do that', I sigh dramatically and march off to look for Steve and Martin in the foyer.

'So much for making up with tradition', Martin laughs.

'There's a chapel here belonging to the sisters, but I don't think they have a service there tonight', Steve says.

We go to the chapel and open its heavy door. The chapel is simple and beautiful with gorgeous icons on the walls. The three of us sit quietly in the building built to the right of Yeshua's house, fully aware of where we are, and we feel the amazing night unfolding ahead of us. Amazing joy. Amazing peace.

On Christmas Day Bernard the middle-aged Frenchman tells me there is going to be a showing of the first-century house under the convent for the French pilgrims. I ask if I can sneak in and he says he is happy to take me along. I've anticipated the moment since our arrival in Nazareth, but the sisters are now very strict with visitors. They show the site only at restricted times. I check the references from *The Urantia Book* Steve has given me. The book describes the house 'as a one-room stone structure with a flat roof and an adjoining building for housing the animals with a "grinding mill" at the back (p.1350)'. Later, when more children were born to Joseph and Mary, they added another room 'which was used as a carpenter's shop' (p.1350). Then I look through the copious materials Steve has given to me before our trip: four small volumes of archaeological data collected on the house by Father Senes between 1936 and 1960, and the papers of Father Livio. As I organise the material, I can't decide whether to put all the information in chronological order or to delve, like an archaeologist, from the most recent times back to the oldest. Father Senes began, like any archaeologist would, with the more recent layers.

The modern story of the house starts on 26 January 1855, when the Sisters of Nazareth moved from France to the Holy Land and bought ten small buildings there. Three years later a workman fell into a cistern about five metres deep, and uncovered a spacious vaulted room and a cave. Gradually other discoveries were made, including the first-century fountain and house as well as a tomb. The first archaeologist to work on the excavations under the convent was Victor Guerin, who in 1885 was introduced to the sisters by the French pilgrim, Father Fulgence. It was Guerin who also sent the sisters an early medieval text by Arculf from 670 CE. Arculf dictated his notes from the Nazareth pilgrimage to Abbot Adamnam. This testimony was well known in the early Middle Ages and was included in a text by Bede circa 720 CE about holy places (*locis sanctis*, 5). A reproduction of it was found in 1157 by Peter Deacon, a librarian at the monastery of Monte Cassino.

Below is Arculf's text as I find it in Senes' and Livio's notes:

> The town of Nazareth, according to Arculf who received hospitality here, has no surrounding wall like Capernaum. Set on a hill, it nevertheless has tall stone buildings. Two very large churches were built there.

The first, in the centre of the town, is constructed over two vaults on the spot where once stood the house in which the Lord our Saviour was brought up. This church, built on two moulds and, as already mentioned, on two interconnected vaults, has beneath it—between the two moulds—a very clear fountain from which the entire population draws water. The water is hoisted to the church above in small vessels by the system of pulleys. The other church was built on the site where once stood the house in which the Archangel Gabriel visited Blessed Mary, whom he found alone and to whom he spoke. We gathered this information about Nazareth from Saint Arculf who received hospitality there two nights and just as many days.

Father Livio's notes also include an earlier testimony translated in the fourth century from Greek into Latin by my old friend Jerome. In the *Onomasticon*, Eusebius wrote about Nazareth:

'There is a church on the site where the angel came to announce the important news to the Blessed Mary, and there is another one on the site where the Lord was brought up'.

Victor Guerin and Abbe Vigoreaux of the Pontifical Biblical Commission concluded, based on the archaeological evidence they found, that the house of the Holy Family was under the Convent of the Sisters of Nazareth. The letter Abbe Vigoreaux sent to Mother Superior on the 1 October 1899 states:

After having carefully examined the localities that you have brought to light, I cannot hold the doubt that you have discovered the sanctuary described by Arculf as having been built on the site of the house of St Joseph:

all the details in his description fit in perfectly with what I have seen.

So how come nobody has known about this before? Okay, the Franciscans built their church on top of what had probably been Mary's house until she married Joseph. Why couldn't the sisters claim they'd found the house in which Yeshua actually lived with his parents, brothers and sisters? First of all, the First World War brought all excavations to a stop. Then the Franciscans claimed they had Mary's house next door to the church. However, the building wasn't old enough to be what they claimed it to be. The sisters didn't want to upset the delicate balance of Christian claims in Nazareth. They had also naively given away most of the artefacts found on the site to the Franciscans.

The excavations recommenced in 1940 with Father Senes who, up until his death in the 1960s, continued excavating the place and eventually reached the same conclusion. He was convinced he had found the house where Yeshua lived. The sisters quietly kept the knowledge to themselves. I suspect they were discouraged from advertising the discovery as it would disclaim the holy sites already 'established' by the Franciscans.

Then along comes the enigmatic Father Silvio. It is a pity I never met him. Steve has a terrible memory of how people look. I would have loved to visit him in Amsterdam. I imagine him as a tall man with dark hair, highly intelligent and curious, but unwilling to shake the establishment. Or perhaps he had been discouraged from doing so?

What he has done for us is to create a tentative chronology of how things happened, which I believe to be very useful.

A house was built near a fountain in the first century—in the era when Yeshua was born. The house, as with the Church of Annunciation on the other side of the road, became a meeting place for early Christians.

Then there was a time gap. In about the fourth century Constantine, the first Christian Roman emperor, started a frenzy of church building in all the known or projected holy places associated with the presence of Yeshua/Jesus. He appointed Count Joseph of Tiberias, a converted Jew, to build two churches in Nazareth: one of the Annunciation and one of the Holy Family/Nutrition. Both churches quickly became places of pilgrimage.

We have the testimonies of Arculf and Eusebius (translated by Jerome) to confirm these events.

In the eighth century, the churches were destroyed with the Islamic expansion and conquest, but the memory of the site of the great Saint buried on the site of the House of the Holy Family lingers in popular memory.

A number of mosques built on the site were destroyed by natural means—probably earthquakes—which made the Islamic clerics believe the Saint buried there was not theirs.

During the eleventh century waves of Christian Crusaders invaded the Holy Land. The Crusaders discovered the remains of an old Christian church on the site and Byzantine Basilica. They considered it a holy place and so left their spurs on the wall in memory of the visit, with a wish to be buried there. They also tried to rebuild a church, but after the battle of Hattin in 1187 they left the Holy Land.

About five centuries pass. The Franciscans came to Nazareth in the seventeenth century. In 1620 a Franciscan called Father Quaresmio wrote that 'at a stone's throw to the north' were the ruins of the Crusaders' church 'which was never built.'

In 1881 the Sisters of Nazareth bought the land. The Sister Superior was told by a man who sold her the land, 'Be careful, my land is on holy ground. This is where the Saint was buried'. Soon after, Guerin (in the 1880s) then Senes (1940-1963) excavated the place and reached the same conclusion.

In October-November 2000 Steve arrived in Nazareth.

In August 2002 Steve went to Amsterdam and met Father Silvio. He obtained all the documents from Father Silvio; that is, the medieval reports, the notes relating to Guerin and Senes, and Father Silvio's own chronology. Steve made two copies of all the documents: one for himself and the other for the sisters.

In December 2005 Steve, Martin and I arrive in Nazareth.

[About a year later, the sisters will decide to employ a full-time archaeologist to work on the site. They will choose a professor of archaeology from the UK].

Who is the Saint who was buried there? The French guide, who takes us to the excavations below the convent, mentions that the tomb is quite possibly that of Joseph, Yeshua's father. Naturally, Joseph would not have been originally buried there. His remains would have been placed there later, after the house had become a place of veneration for early Christians. Even centuries later, it was known that the ground was somehow holy and it was assumed that a Saint must have been buried there.

Throughout the tour the guide keeps repeating that the sisters can't claim 100 per cent that this is Joseph's house, where young Yeshua lived, and that all we know about the place is that it was built in the first century and by the end of the century it had already become a venerated place and was considered sacred. Next door with their tickets, the Franciscans believe the house under their church is the one where the Annunciation took place.

I don't care for the Annunciation simply because it is too bizarre for me and smells of the sort of common legend every religious tradition claims before the birth of a great being. Apparently Buddha's mother was also visited by an angel who more or less told her the same story. These kinds of details don't interest me—I consider them too 'mythological' for my tastes. I don't have the same propensity for detail that drives Steve either. I just want to feel the place where Yeshua lived: the street where he walked, the threshold he stepped over, a wall which he leaned on and laughed at as a boy. I want to see the kitchen where he ate, and the room where he slept and dreamed as a child. I want to feel it all.

The tour guide is explaining the archaeological details of the rooms, the cistern, the naves and columns, and the layers of other buildings above. Archaeological details are always a weird maze to me, but the previous readings of the site's archaeological notes help me—I can take in everything the guide says almost unconsciously, and so concentrate on the feeling of the place. The tour guide answers my last question though: he believes the tomb near the house is the place where Joseph, Yeshua's father, was buried by early Christians. This isn't a regular Jewish custom. However, after Yeshua's death the early Christian community decided to make a shrine of the house and bury his father there. It is convincing enough for me. I love the place and its energy.

I breathe in the peace of the place full with the possibility of Yeshua's early presence—the great being who was born into a normal family and achieved his full spiritual potential as a human being, as a divine being, and as a man, inspiring others to reach beyond their human condition and its limitations.

For a moment I stand on the threshold to the house. Once inside, I have the feeling I am visiting a misunderstood friend with whom I want to make peace. Two thousand years of complications and political power games between us are nothing. They are not him, and they are not me. For a moment in his house I feel his peace clearing away my inner turmoil.

I go straight to Steve's room to share my impressions of the place. In the courtyard, Jonathan is walking reminiscent of Modigliani in nervous circles in his long, black bohemian coat, and he asks me whether I have a cigarette.

TRAVELS

The next day Martin and I walk to Nazareth Village, which is supposed to be a reconstruction of Nazareth from Yeshua's time. The two of us walk through polluted, noisy streets until we arrive at the gate of the village, only to learn it isn't open that day, or it might be open later, but no one knows at what time.

Even the woman in the souvenir shop belonging to the museum doesn't know if it will be open. We browse through different souvenirs. I buy a few books on Nazareth and reproductions of tiny oil lamps used in Yeshua's time. Strangely, I am not particularly disappointed. The place, as it is now, does not inspire me at all. Perhaps the long walk along the busy streets and traffic has spoiled the feeling.

We walk back to the nunnery where Steve, who does not seem at all surprised the village isn't open, announces that in that case we will grab a taxi and go to Sepphoris.

'Sepphoris will give you what the village didn't', he says.

The three of us walk out of the convent and back to a little street lined with endless souvenir shops. Kolya, a woman from Tel Aviv who owns a shop here, immediately recognises Steve from his previous trips and finds us a taxi. With bright-gold eye-shadow and bleached orange-yellow hair, Kolya looks like some ancient Aztec entity in the midst of Nazareth's kitsch. The taxi driver, her 'most trusted friend', is a baby-faced, bulky man who has never heard of Sepphoris in his life, but insists he knows how to get there.

I look back at Kolya with eyebrows raised.

'Just believe me, girl. He knows the way—and if he doesn't, he can call me and I'll direct him', she reassures me with confidence.

We begin a confused journey around Nazareth, with the driver telling us we are going in the 'general direction' of Sepphoris. About an hour later we finally turn onto the right road to the excavations. Sepphoris is a first-century Jewish Roman town and, according to tradition, is considered the birthplace of Anne, Mary's mother and Yeshua's grandmother. I am charmed by the town. The remaining road and the elegant sidewalks leading to villas with delicate mosaics called 'Amazon', 'Dionysus, Ariadne' and 'Orpheus' show the artistry of the Roman town. The tower over the hills provides spectacular vistas of Galilee which, apart from a few new developments in the distance, would not have changed much from Yeshua's times. There is also a beautiful old synagogue that Yeshua might have visited. New scholarship takes this possibility into account.

Sepphoris is not mentioned in the Bible, but it is given an elaborate description in *The Urantia Book* as the place where young Yeshua worked for six months. According to the book, Joseph, his father, died in Sepphoris while working on a construction site. You can imagine young Yeshua here, in the busy daily life of this Romanised town in Galilee, walking its boulevards with their magnificent mosaics, watching the traffic. The town also gives a more sophisticated touch to Yeshua's life, as he was exposed to this beautiful town only a few kilometres from Nazareth. You can see him here talking to craftsmen and artists; maybe even arguing with local scholars and visiting poets with the passion of a young and brilliant man. The Jesus of the Bible has always been an inaccessible figure for me, full of hideous suffering which horrified me. But in Sepphoris I catch a glimpse of him as a young man contemplating his future as it was revealed to him. I can see it with his eyes, as a fulfilment of his destiny.

There is nothing in the Bible about Jesus' years between his teaching at the Temple of Jerusalem as a young boy, to his adult years as a seasoned spiritual teacher. This gap alone should have made me suspicious.

I have never treated *The Urantia Book* as *the* source, and I was never its follower. When Steve gave me the book, I considered it an additional source, a 'gap filler'—and I still think of it that way. If I find a better source, I'll turn to it. Spiritual teachings have been transmitted to humanity via inspired human beings for millennia. Each religious tradition has its great teachers, prophets and enlightened ones. Great religious texts have been dictated throughout human history or, as some legends claim, found under rocks fully written. Moses had to go to the mountain to bring back the teachings; Muhammad was in a holy trance when God spoke to him. The messages were perhaps pure, but what was transmitted went through socially conditioned human minds, often caught up in the ethos of the times. Perhaps the man who claimed *The Urantia Book* had been dictated to him in his sleep was also such a source. I have no problem with that.

In *The Urantia Book*, Yeshua went to Sepphoris at the age of twenty-two. The carpentry trade in Nazareth was slow and, being a dutiful son, he went to Sepphoris to learn to be a smith. The picture painted in the book is that of a perfect son. I prefer to think of young Yeshua as looking forward to this adventure in the big city, where the Romanised Jewish population lived and mingled freely with the Gentiles.

Did he look at women as they walked seductively to the baths in their sandals and loosely wrapped togas? Did he go to the baths? Or was he a young ascetic man, as some interpretations of the Dead Sea Scrolls would have it? I ponder the question a little. Sepphoris was a sophisticated town where Herod Antipas occasionally resided. It was the capital of Galilee, with grand avenues paved with colourful mosaics and graceful columns showcasing some of the best workmanship in the Roman Empire. It was where gossip was exchanged in the baths and elegant people cruised theatres at night and markets during the day. In many ways, Sepphoris wasn't very different from any other provincial capital of the Roman Empire. It was powerful, decadent and beautiful. Why would an ascetic young man come here? More likely, a brilliant young man with a great vision of life had come here the way any young person might today go from a small town to the closest city—to explore the possibilities the city could offer. *A natural thing to do.* So yes, I imagine he did look at women and perhaps smiled at their vanity as they walked gracefully by wearing too much make-up, laughing seductively at the curious young man from a small town.

What happened after Sepphoris? If I could dream Yeshua's life I would say he went travelling. What is it about travel that is so soul-renewing, so rejuvenating, so life-giving? Now and then I ask myself why I left Poland. I am always clear in my mind I am not a migrant because I didn't migrate for economic reasons.

Economics has never motivated me in my life choices. It would have been so much easier to stay there: within a short time I would have had a successful academic career as a lecturer in philosophy, as well as a few books published. It would be so much easier to write in my first language than in English, my third language. I had already been published there and had been asked to submit a full-length manuscript. So why did I leave? I left because I had no choice. According to my inner predisposition, I was a traveller and a stranger. I had to leave. By leaving I was following my natural inclination to explore the world. To learn my personal destiny, the same way that some people follow their careers or live for their family. I followed mine. It helped me understand that I flowed with the natural rhythm of the energy of my life.

Eventually even the novelty of travel wears off. I heard a story once told by a spiritual teacher about his friend who loved travelling and felt happy in every new place. For a while. Then, inevitably, six or seven months after arriving, the old anxiety, boredom and frustrations would kick in and he would have to move on to yet another place. I know that I am that friend. In the end, travel and new places are only vehicles for the renewal of our senses. Depending on your connection to a place, geographical romance with a new location can last from six to eighteen months (very much like the ecstasy of human romance) before weariness returns. However, my wanderlust isn't about the travel alone. It isn't about new places. It is about the renewal of the soul, about the return to the senses, the ability to feel and experience beauty, love, joy, wisdom and bliss. The bliss. Travel is one way of getting it. Sex is another. So is meditation. In time I want to grow spiritually enough to have that bliss always: even when in one place, even when I am somewhere forever.

Yeshua too must have searched for wisdom and bliss. Bliss, after all, is an aspect of Peace—Yeshua's favourite word. Apart from sparse references to the episode in Jerusalem when, as a young boy, he amazed the rabbis with his wisdom, there is very little evidence in the Bible of Yeshua's intellectual abilities. *The Urantia Book* creates a picture of a young, learned man, who was a favourite of his teachers. I find this characterisation of him too one-dimensional. Just because he was a brilliant student doesn't mean he didn't disobey anybody. If he were human, he must have had moments of weakness—we all have them. But I can easily accept an image of him as an intelligent young man who believed he had a special destiny. Being aware of his mission and his gifts, he must have been eager to explore them intellectually. *The Urantia Book* also mentions that in his early twenties he received invitations to become a teacher in the great learning centres of that age, Damascus and Alexandria. But he rejected them. A few years later, at the age of twenty-eight, he met some Indian merchants, a father and a son, and travelled through the Mediterranean world with them. He visited Rome, Athens, Crete, Carthage, Caesarea, Antioch, Alexandria, Crete and even Mesopotamia.

Hmmm . . . Young Yeshua, the learned, tenacious man in Jerusalem, meeting merchants from the East. I imagine they met in one of the eateries in the Old City which now sit almost unchanged on the Palestinian side, hidden in the crevices of Old Jerusalem. Men sitting at the tables eating hummus with salads and meats.

> The entrance is a small arch in the wall. To walk in, you need to bend a little and, here, immediately, the rest of the place is fully visible; suddenly much bigger than it appeared to be from the outside, with ten, or even twenty, wooden tables filled with people dressed in white. A couple of waiters move around in a very

efficient and inviting way. A young Yeshua walks in, looks around for a familiar table or face, and sits at one of the tables. The Indian merchant and his son are just finishing their meal and cannot help but notice the young man. The merchant waves to the waiter and asks him about Yeshua. He wants to be introduced.

His interpreter, the merchant explains, cannot follow him on his journeys anymore. Would he, Yeshua, be interested in the job?

'Where are you going?' Yeshua asks.

'Rome, Alexandria, Athens', the exotic man answers.

Rome, Alexandria, Athens . . . these names must have been a sweet sound to a young man. The sound of adventure and learning. Perhaps even some answers about his own destiny. The curiosity of a young mind about other great teachings.

This is where the question of divinity reappears: if Yeshua were a divine being, did he still have anything to learn? In all traditions, the great beings fully accessed their divine capacities *within* their human potential. They experienced their divinity as part of that potential. Whether they were incarnated, that is, divine beings who took on human bodies, or human beings who reached their divine destinies, they still lived within the human body and mind. They faced their limitations and broke through them. But they operated within them and were aware of them, as well as being aware of the possibility of transcending them.

When I was studying philosophy I was perplexed about the whole mixture of divinity and humanity in Jesus. The myths and fairy tales I was asked to believe didn't work for me. The endless number of church synods on the topic proved only that the Church itself was weary of the idea. A great number of 'heretics' have been denounced depending on what they happened to think about the ratio of the divine to human in Jesus. When I left Toronto I was already looking for another way to relate to God. I was already a seeker. Until then I had only been an intellectual seeker—a bit of an intellectual eccentric—who, instead of studying the popular philosophers of the twentieth century or getting involved in more sought-after subjects such as bioethics, was fascinated by the esoteric teachings of the Middle Ages. Life supported me in that personal obsession, as I was offered one scholarship after another to follow my passion. I was an intellectual seeker because this was the only way I knew how to seek.

Then, very reluctantly, I was introduced to Eastern philosophies. I say reluctantly because I believed the West was so highly intellectually cultivated that it would have been obscene and unwise to look for wisdom elsewhere. When a friend introduced me to Zen, I was shocked. From the Zen point of view, all my intellectualism was not an asset to relish but an obstacle. I intended to be outraged by that preposterous idea, but strangely, I wasn't. Zen was too interesting and too challenging to discredit. Haiku poetry was a revelation. So was the realisation that in Eastern traditions the concept of sin didn't exist. Sin was not an evil act, but an 'act of ignorance', and thus it could be easily redeemed through proper understanding. One insight after another followed and I became hooked: I began reading the *Vedanta* (the Hindu Scriptures). I also bought all the Buddhist writings I could find and devoured them, one by one. Many spoke of practice and meditation. If western theology is speculation about God, the Eastern approach is more about methodology.

Like a maniac, I began getting up at four in the morning to do breathing exercises and to teach myself meditation. My first husband became seriously irritated. At the time I was working as a substitute teacher in Toronto high schools and experiencing nervous breakdowns on a daily basis. I hated my job. I hated it once I discovered that 'teaching' wasn't about shared learning but about controlling rioting teenagers who didn't want to be there. The kids screamed and rebelled, and I kept at my meditation. Outside the window the sky was low with autumn beauty, but I was too cloudy to notice it. The maple trees yelled with yellow, red and brown rainbows of leaves, but I was barely aware of them. The leaves danced gently to the ground, squeaking under the students' feet, but I didn't hear them.

I saw writing on the walls of the classroom that no one could read but me: 'She is dreaming of passion and far-away countries.'

At night I lay next to my husband dreaming about running away to Mexico, baking in the sun, having passionate affairs, and writing. But life has its own design. As I was musing about Mexico, I received an invitation to teach at an Australian university in Southeast Asia.

'Strange', I thought, 'how you want one thing and get another'. As soon as I arrived there and left my husband behind, I was consumed by a desire to find a guru. I listened to many teachers and learned what they had to say. Apart from the lack of the notion of sin, the most interesting thing for me was the concept of enlightenment. I began to think that perhaps Yeshua was an enlightened being. Someone who, through spiritual inclination and practice, becomes permanently connected with God. The Hindus also have a concept of incarnation: the avatar is a god who takes a human body to come back to earth and teach us higher truths.

In a way, whether great beings like Yeshua were incarnated or whether they were humans who achieved divinity is not really important. On a higher level, it is one and the same thing—the distinction is important only to scholastic theologians. Great beings don't come here to be worshipped. They come here to show us *the way* to become what they are. They want to show us *the method* so we can fulfil our own potential. We build them altars when we don't understand them, or as a reminder that we too can be divine. Time and time again, they come here and teach us. Time and time again, we forget the lessons. We are annoyingly slow.

Alternatively, in western non-religious sources Yeshua is often portrayed as a political figure caught up in the politics of the time. I doubt this. Being who he was, I think he had very little interest in politics, in its passing importance. I imagine him as more open-minded, capable of going beyond local politics. All great beings are. They have a vision of the unity of the world, which at times might not be easily accessible to us, but is always there for them. A vision of Peace and Unity. No, I don't think Yeshua was political at all—especially in any nationalistic way. That would be grotesque. But we all imagine him differently. My grandfather thought Yeshua, with his bent for equality, was the first communist. For me, he was a traveller and a scholar.

Rome, Alexandria, Athens . . . For Yeshua, travel was an opportunity to see the world, to witness people's lives outside the narrow parametres of his daily experiences. These places were treasures of knowledge in the ancient world. Alexandria was established in northern Egypt in 334 BCE by Alexander the Great. The city became the centre of learning in the Hellenistic world: no ship was allowed to leave its port until all the books it carried were copied by the scribes of the Alexandrian Library. Soon Alexandria would boast of possessing all the known sources of knowledge, housed in its library. Great astronomers, builders, philosophers lived there. The most famous of these was a Hellenised Jewish philosopher called Philo of Alexandria. 'Hellenised' meaning he wrote and taught in Greek. Intellectually he was a Greek philosopher, even though he was Jewish by religion. This wasn't unusual in Alexandria. In the first century CE Alexandria had been, culturally and intellectually, what New York became in the second part of the twentieth century. As a philosopher, Philo was a follower of Plato, whom he revered. Scholars agree that his intention was to create a link between the religious teachings of the Hebrew tradition and Greek philosophical thought.

If we are to believe in the narrative of Yeshua's journeys in *The Urantia Book*, then Yeshua did visit Alexandria with his Indian benefactors, but did not meet Philo, who was apparently sick at the time. This was one of the more unfortunate mischances in human history. Had they met in Alexandria or Jerusalem—where Philo travelled on occasion—they could have had a dialogue of utmost importance. Their meeting could have potentially helped prevent the Judeo-Christian schism which occurred after Yeshua's death. The rest of Yeshua's travels continued throughout the Mediterranean, where in different cities he had the chance to meet a colourful array of people with whom he held philosophical discussions. His erudition earned him the name of the 'Damascus scribe' or 'Jewish tutor'.

The Urantia Book is not the only source which fills in the gaps of Yeshua's early years. The most notable other example comes from a late nineteenth-century Russian doctor, Nicolai Notovich. Notovich travelled through Punjab and northern India, mostly Kashmir. He broke his leg in the city of Leh and was moved to a Buddhist monastery in Himis. While recovering, he discovered *The Life of St Issa*, which in every aspect recalls the life of Jesus. The text speaks of a travelling Saint who taught laws identical to the ten commandments, spoke against the caste system, taught love for one's neighbour, referred to Moses, and proclaimed himself to be an Israelite.

He also performed healing miracles reluctantly and taught in the temples.

The latter part of the story speaks of St Issa's trial at the hands of Pilate, resolving any doubt as to what the document refers to. According to Notovich's source, Yeshua left his home at the age of thirteen when it was time for him to choose a wife. He snuck out of the house and travelled to the East with some merchants. Once in India he visited the holy city of Benares, as well as going to Kashmir and Nepal, where he taught about the Eternal Spirit and listened to eastern sages. No doubt there are inconsistencies here between the two sources. In *The Urantia Book* young Yeshua began his journeys in his twenties, while Notovich's source claims he left in his early teens. However, there is something connecting the two sources: the claim that Yeshua was a wisdom-seeker. The compassionate teachings of Yeshua, which seemed completely out of touch with his times, were already being practised by the Buddhists in the East. That he encountered them there and they confirmed his own intuitions and revelations makes perfect sense. When Notovich brought *The Life of St Issa* to the West he sparked a controversy. Many questioned the validity of the source, and some travelled back to Kashmir to prove their point.

The name 'Issa' and its derivatives are often associated with Jesus in the East. In Islam, Jesus is known as *Issar* or *Yuz Azaf*. Islamic sources are even more controversial—they question Yeshua's death on the cross and tell the story of his travels to the East after he escaped crucifixion. A German writer, Holger Kersten, recently published a book which sets out to prove that Jesus travelled through India *during* his early adulthood *and after* his crucifixion. In *Jesus Lived in India*, Kersten argues—along with some Muslim and Hindu scholars—that the true tomb of Jesus is in Kashmir, in the town of Srinagar.

Some Christian Gnostic sources talk about Yeshua's life after the crucifixion as well. The Acts of Thomas and The Gospel of Thomas refer to a meeting between Yeshua and Thomas in Anatolia some time after the crucifixion, where Yeshua orders Thomas to go to India. *The Urantia Book*, on the other hand, claims it was another apostle, Nathaniel, who was sent to India to spread the teachings.

The appearances of Yeshua to his disciples after his crucifixion are an integral part of Christian scriptures. The question here is whether he appeared to them as a spirit or as a human being who had survived the ordeal of crucifixion. The possibility that Yeshua lived *after* the crucifixion would be very upsetting to many people, and disastrous for many churches. Some years ago this possibility would have unsettled me as well. Was he really the Son of God if he wasn't miraculously resurrected? None of these stories cause me any anxiety now, as I believe Yeshua's presence in our lives has always been about his life and teachings, and not about how he died or whether he was resurrected. The essence of the story of Yeshua isn't about getting his body back after death, but about fulfilling his divine destiny and his human spiritual potential. Having said that, I'm a little doubtful about Yeshua's travels after the crucifixion. The gnostic sources especially have difficulty dealing with the death of the Teacher and look for ways to save Yeshua from that part of his destiny. I don't want to discredit the stories solely because they are often inconsistent in their details. They tell an intriguing story which might include some truth. However, I can't help but feel that for me this part of Yeshua's story sounds a little bit like the 'Elvis was here!' tales. Often when a charismatic figure dies they are spotted in the most unusual places and situations. I'm much more at ease with Yeshua's travels during his young adulthood.

When I travelled through Asia and spoke to Hindu gurus, I was surprised that many of them also venerated Jesus and that they too believed he travelled extensively in his young adulthood and came to India as part of his travels. In Malaysia, for example, I met Raja, a young man in his late twenties who had practiced yoga since he could remember and who became my yoga teacher. He and his wife were *Sanyasis*, celibate renunciants, who ran an ashram in the suburb of Kuala Lumpur and took care of disabled people. Raja's house was dilapidated and always full of people who either needed help or wanted to give help. As with many suburban places in Kuala Lumpur, it was situated near a small, neglected park. The heat and humidity were omnipresent. The house was decrepit, the park was neglected—but nature took care of both. Flowers always bloomed in the park and the jasmine bushes and bougainvilleas exploded with colour and scent. It was messy and unstoppable. At the centre of the house-turned-ashram lived an old bedridden woman. Everyone showed her the highest regard and went to get her blessing.

'Who is she and what's wrong with her?' I asked Raja once.

He looked at me, surprised, and said, 'There is nothing wrong with her. She is a self-realised being who has willingly taken on the karma of the people around her and', he circled his arms, 'the rest of the world. Like Jesus'.

I immediately liked Raja. He puzzled me. There was a quiet dignity about him. When I saw him walking to a yoga class dressed all in white with a pony tail, I thought, 'A postmodern yogi'. But there was more than that to Raja. His yoga classes included intense breathing exercises and esoteric meditation practices. One day after class I asked him, 'Who is *your* guru, Raja?'

'I am glad you asked', he said. 'Jesus Christ.'

'You're not a Hindu?'

He looked at me as if I had just suffered an episode of mental retardation, for which he was going to forgive me that one time. 'I am a Hindu, but I am also "Merry Christmas"', he answered with conviction. 'Jesus was a great yogi. He came to India when he was young and achieved yoga—union with God. After that he went back home to teach his own people.'

That was interesting, I thought, but I didn't seek any more answers for a while.

Occasionally I went to talks given by Indian gurus who were visiting Kuala Lumpur. One guru caught my attention. I read in the local papers about his arrival from India to give lectures on Vedanta. The hall in which he was to give the lectures was in the Indian Quarter—a part of Kuala Lumpur I didn't know well. It was a late-evening lecture and the taxi drove me through tiny, dark alleys with hardly any street lamps. I was horrified when the driver declared he couldn't find the street, but that 'it should be in the area', and left me at the gate of something which looked like an abandoned street market. Small Indian children, no older than six years of age, immediately appeared around me. I gave them the name of the street and they guided me to an old theatre where the lecture was taking place. The Vedantin guru had quite a following. The old, two-hundred-seat theatre was filled with respectful listeners—all of them Hindu except me. I felt like a walking white ghost as their eyes turned to me with surprise.

Always the good student, I sat in the first row. When the guru lectured, he sat crossed-legged, all in white, tall, disciplined and magnificent. He spoke of the path of wisdom. 'Do what you need to do', he said 'and surrender the fruits of your work to the divine. Don't worry about the results. Don't worry about the opinions of others, about the praise or blame that may or may not come. This is a true renunciation—the renunciation of the fruits of your actions, but not of action itself'.

It appealed to the scholar in me.

I listened.

'Subdue your senses to the intellect so that the Atman, the Spirit, will fully manifest in you', he continued with his teachings.

Subdue your senses?! He got me there. I raised my hand and asked, 'What about other experiences in life: love, career, relationships?'

He looked at me. His eyes were very clear—doubtless the eyes of a man who had surpassed all his doubts. 'Only the intellect is the right path. The rest are only distractions from the search for the Highest Truth. Vedanta is That', he said with great conviction.

'What about God?' I asked again under his icy gaze.

'God is the Absolute', he said. 'God is the ultimate reality and the only reality. The rest is an illusion. The whole created world is an illusion, the deceiving *maya*. Once you gain the understanding through the right teaching, you will realise it. You will live it.'

I wasn't sure. It reminded me too much of a punishing asceticism, an unhealthy denial of the sensual aspects of life that traditional religions often propagate.

After the lecture I approached him and asked him about Jesus.

'Was he a yogi?'

The Brahmin looked at me with amusement. 'He had to be a yogi to attain the Wisdom and teach it to his people. First he met Patanjali, and later he was trained by the Brahmins.'

I went home and checked my dates. Patanjali was a yogi sage who wrote the *Yoga Sutras* and lived some time between 200 BCE and 100 CE. Theoretically, he and Yeshua could both have lived at the same time. Perhaps they even met; that is, if Yeshua did go to India. I must say I liked the Hindu take on Yeshua's story. Whenever you are lucky enough to meet beings of great spiritual calibre, you learn very fast that they don't care for religions or names. This alone was a significant distinction between the truly great teachers and the ones who only aspired to be like them. The truly great teachers are non sectarian even if, by birth or choice, they operate within certain religious traditions. Traditions are cultural and created by people. The mystic understanding of life and God isn't constrained by such uniquely human limitations.

I would like to believe in the possibility that the two men, both spiritual giants, met in India or Mesopotamia. They would have had so much in common. At first, perhaps, they might have looked at each other with suspicion and curiosity, but soon they would have seen similarities. Young Yeshua would have recognised the inner bliss of the yogi. He would have known the feeling of the mysterious connection with the divine, even if he didn't use the same methods. As a manifestation of God, Yeshua was the personification of what Patanjali was writing about: achievement of the inner state of connection with the Self. The Self, God, the Father—they are all the same. Young Yeshua would have approached the meditating Patanjali, trying so hard to 'still the waves of the mind' and to remove himself from the world to join the Imperishable Brahman. He would have wondered at the ascetic methods of self-discipline Patanjali imposed on himself to reach inner peace. In no other place but India could one see the passing of life and our anxious and desperate efforts to hold on to our bodies, our lives, our belonging, our loved ones—as if it were possible to do so successfully. In India one sees the passing of lives like clouds in the sky.

'I see everything as a witness, but I am not involved in any of that. I do what I am asked to do by my karma and perform my duties as is expected of me, but I know that I am not those duties, I am not that social persona, I am not that life. Beneath all of these, I am the Self', Patanjali would have said to young Yeshua.

'Yes', young Yeshua would have agreed. 'The Spirit. Underneath all our masks we are the Spirit. Peace be with you.'

I believe they would have nodded in recognition of each other's states and exchanged some methods. What a powerful lesson for those of us who look for separation and conflict, rather than similarities or even sameness! Despite my love for the city, I know Jerusalem is the most pathological example of conflict. Sameness in spirit rather than separateness of cultural details . . . Why is it so hard?

I want to believe in the story of Yeshua's explorations in India. It is a good story. I am happy with this filling of the gap in Yeshua's life and how it made his life more adventurous and less painful. I can't bear the grotesque images of bleeding Christs on the altars of Catholic churches. I like Jesus being a little more adventurous, having some fun from time-to-time—like turning water into wine at a wedding or going off to India. Enough of his suffering and torment.

Let him travel and see the world before he brings his message to us. Let him travel . . .

THE SEA OF GALILEE

We decide it is time to leave the hills of Nazareth, Yeshua's house and the terrible pollution and traffic of the town. Steve and Martin have planned it so the next step on our pilgrimage is the Sea of Galilee. It is the morning of 27 December and we pack our suitcases, have a quick breakfast in the sisters' dining room and walk to the bus station. We struggle with our suitcases through the town's heavy traffic, then wait for about half an hour for the bus to Tiberias. Steve is visibly relieved and excited about going to Tiberias. Even Martin, who doesn't like to show much excitement (although he has fallen victim to occasional bouts of 'Jerusalem fever'), is in high spirits.

It is a beautiful, sunny day. The bus isn't air-conditioned; the air is hot and numbing, so I sleep through the fifty-minute journey to Tiberias. Vaguely I remember Martin pointing out the 'Cana' sign—the place where Yeshua performed one of my favourite miracles: changing water into wine. I am too dazed to notice whether we are actually passing by the town or have just seen the sign showing the way to Cana.

'That's interesting', I mumble, and return to my sleepy stupor caused by the combination of hot weather and the smell of gasoline. The bus is full—mostly of Palestinians, I guess. I observe that Nazareth is inhabited by Palestinians while Tiberias is primarily Jewish. The idiosyncrasies of the Holy Land.

I wake up as the bus is meandering through the streets of Tiberias. Compared to Nazareth and especially Jerusalem, Tiberias presents itself like a resort town. Traffic is present, but there is a certain freshness in the air, a different quality of light. I later learn that Tiberias was established in the first twenty years CE by Herod Antipas and was named after the Roman Emperor Tiberius. Not surprisingly, it has always been a spa town, as there are a number of hot springs in the area. In the fourth century Tiberias was home to a famous Talmudic school. And a great medieval philosopher, Moses Maimonides, was buried there. The Crusaders of the eleventh century took an interest in the town and built many churches there, as they did nearly everywhere else. No doubt the Sea of Galilee and its association with Yeshua's most prolific years was attractive to them.

The history of the Holy Land is similar in every area. There would be a Muslim presence for several centuries and then, with the establishment of Jewish quarters in the nineteenth century, a town would experience a second birth and prosperity. A complex but repetitive history: the Romans would establish a town, great Jewish scholars and lawyers would move in, then Christian Crusaders would come and build churches. The Crusaders lost the Battle of Hattin in 1187, and the Sultan of Egypt slaughtered the Christian populations and built mosques. The wise Suleiman rebuilt the town and the Jewish population slowly returned, bringing back affluence and synagogues. And so the story went in loops: battles shedding blood over a Holy Land, which for some exotic reason could belong to only one religion at a time. Yes, reading the history of the Holy Land is like wandering in endless repetitive circles.

Again we walk through the streets with our suitcases, but this time they don't feel very heavy. Perhaps the possibility of a new adventure is lifting us. This time we also know where we are staying—the same place Steve and Martin stayed on their previous trips, the Franciscan hospice of Casa Nova. The main attraction of the hospice is its location right on the Sea of Galilee with a terrace overlooking the 'Sea', although now trees partially block the view.

The Sea of Galilee has a poetic history. It is also called Lake Kinneret, as it forms a big concentration of fresh water in a very dry land. The word 'kinnor' in Hebrew means 'harp': a musical instrument producing very sweet sounds. The whole sea is said to carry the sounds of Yeshua's teachings. Geographically, it is about twenty-one kilometres long, thirteen kilometres wide and over two hundred metres below sea level.

The rooms of the Casa Nova are large, if austere. A big old bed with an iron bed-head in the middle of the room, short, white window curtains and an old closet. I throw myself on the bed, trying to process what has happened to me on the trip so far. I am lucky—both men have planned everything for me, have already been to places I am now seeing, and are the most amazing guides and friends. Friends. 'Friends' is Steve's favourite word. 'Lover' is a word he would rather avoid, and 'wife' is something that brings bad memories.

What is Martin's favourite word? 'Favourite' is itself not a word Martin would use lightly. Martin is too logical to construct someone or something as his favourite. 'Family' is the word he uses most often and it means the world to him. Martin is about family. After family comes friends, and I feel very privileged that this quiet, subdued man now considers me his friend and is there for me as I fall through my personal dramas. He doesn't pretend he understands them or can relate to them. He has enough grace and compassion in him not to judge me. He mentions in passing that he only witnesses 'the immense suffering you are going through on this trip'. He witnesses how every day I pull myself up from it, rising to the adventure and our companionship every morning. He sits quietly by my side as I write frantically in my journals. I carry two journals during the trip: an official journal—which is my guide for this book— and an unofficial one, in which I am processing my feelings. Martin, a friend, is there for me when I feel like I am dying of emotional pain and confusion. He is there for me in his quiet presence.

What are *my* favourite words then?

Lover, adventurer, writer, pilgrim.

Funny how we define ourselves through the words we repeat.

Even in my pain I can see I have been living the words I love. And that, of itself, is beautiful compensation for the momentary suffering I feel.

In the afternoon we walk to the left of the hospice and enjoy the view of the hills all around the sea. These are the places Yeshua visited frequently, traversed daily, as a Teacher.

'I wanted you to come here', Steve says to me as we sit on one of the rocks on the beach, with Martin looking for shells on the shore. 'This place isn't about Yeshua's death. It's not about his suffering. It's not about blame and carrying guilt. These hills and lake are about his happy years—about the fulfilment of his destiny as a great spiritual teacher who wanted us to achieve what he achieved spiritually. These were his happy years, when he walked with his devoted disciples along these hills, taught in the synagogues, met his apostles, left his trail as a Teacher.'

I breathe out heavily. This is exactly what I need to hear as far as my relationship with Yeshua is concerned. If I can't relate to the gory images of a suffering man-God in Catholic churches, or the gruesome processions to commemorate his suffering during the Easter celebrations, I can relate to Yeshua as a maturing Teacher. A man young in years, but possessing great spiritual insight and depth as a Teacher. A man loved by his friends and disciples. A man who chose an alternative destiny: he could have married, had a family and job, but chose otherwise. He knew the priority of inner growth. He knew how important it was that we connect with God through love and compassion. *My Peace I give.* A man who wanted us to feel the inner Peace that is available to us, if we only make the effort to look with innocent eyes—beyond our desires, fear and anger, beyond conditioned minds telling us what we need to do to be happy only to leave us with dust in our mouths. He wanted us to be grand, to rejoice in our magnificent destiny as God's children. Here, in the hills around the Sea of Galilee, he taught these truths.

I gradually feel more peaceful as we walk back past the cafes stretched along the shore. This is a place to celebrate life. Steve and I have two enormous cappuccinos topped with whipped cream. Martin goes to the Internet cafe to check if there is a message from the lawyers in Tel Aviv.

'Guess what?' Martin exclaims. 'Shmuel Yaari's invited us for dinner at his place on Sunday.'

'And the lawyers?'

'The lawyers want to meet us on Monday at 6.30 pm in Tel Aviv on 30 December. And . . .'

'And?'

'They've given us fifteen per cent discount on their fees, since it's not a "commercial" case.'

Steve smiles. 'Let's celebrate over dinner.'

I like that part of Steve's personality: always finding a reason for celebration. The smallest pretext, a tiny piece of good news calls for a good dinner . . . on him.

The sun is setting on the sea. At its centre a boat full of young people is pumping out rap music—surreal in the quiet of the afternoon.

On the way back to the hospice I notice a small old church and go inside. It is a beautiful eleventh-century chapel built by the Crusaders in 1099. On the nave above the altar is a very simple and sweet mosaic of St Peter's boat. There are two other people in the chapel: an American man in his late thirties and an older-looking, extremely cheerful (to the point of irritation) woman.

They greet us as 'brothers and sisters', which freaks me out a little. I hate belonging to any club, especially a religious club, and the last thing I want on this trip is to be identified as part of some sect or religion. Right from the start of our journey we agreed this was about our personal connection with Yeshua, even if, in my case, the connection was non-existent at that stage. It wasn't about preaching, claiming anything or proving anyone wrong. This was a strictly personal journey for seeking spiritual connection with a great being. But over and over again we are put in situations where we are asked to declare ourselves, or worse, assumptions are made about our religious convictions.

When Martin makes an executive decision for us to stay for the service, I feel frustrated and rebellious. I can feel a mean little girl in me stamping her feet, screaming, 'You've ruined my experience. I want to be alone here with St Peter'.

A young Argentinean priest comes out all smiles and performs a rudimentary service for the five of us: some readings from the Scriptures and no nonsense. A simple teaching about the healing of forgiveness. No letters from the bishop asking for donations or denouncing condoms and abortion. I breathe more easily after the first five minutes. Despite his small audience, the young priest is enthusiastic. He must have some American Indian blood in him as his skin has a lovely golden-bronze hue.

The only other time I have participated in a service this simple was at Mt Currie in Canada's British Columbia. It was in a small church near a Native Indian reserve, where another young priest with a Spanish accent tried to do his best for a small group of people one Sunday morning. It is refreshing to see a church and a priest without the pomp and self-righteousness I associate with the institution now. The simplicity of the service is in line with what Steve has previously said about Yeshua's teaching around the Sea of Galilee.

I relax and try to remember the words of prayers I haven't used for a long while and which I originally learned in Polish anyway. Steve is bedazzled and looks like a schoolboy who has walked into the wrong class and has been asked to take a test. Of the three of us, Martin does best: he knows all the prayers by heart and all the right moves. When to sit down and when to get up. I watch him closely and mimic him when I am not sure. Steve does what he can, considering he has never attended a Catholic mass before. He is relieved when Martin and I approach him.

'We can go now, Steve.'

The two Americans turn out to be a preacher-in-training and an eighty-four year old nun. I decide immediately that the preacher-in-training is a total jerk—not through any fault on his part, except that he is a preacher-in-training, which is enough to turn me off. I imagine him as a future TV preacher, hitting people on their foreheads while screaming 'Hallelujah!', and charging them for his services in order to build some crazy shelter filled with guns in case the end of the world comes sometime soon. Okay, perhaps I get a little carried away. Is that some leftover Catholic snobbery in me? I don't know. Apparently he is a recovered bad boy who has fallen in love with a Jesus girl back in Kansas City. On their first date she asks him, 'Do you love Jesus, Tom?'

'Sure', he says, just in case. The rest is history. She signs him up to Alcoholics Anonymous and forbids him to visit hookers. Soon they get married and he becomes committed to the cause of teaching in the Holy Land.

'I don't need it in my book', I mumble, irritated, as he tells me his story after the service. 'I don't need it. I'm not one of you.'

As for the nun—I can't be angry with her. She belongs to an extremely strict meditative order which doesn't allow its nuns any contact with the world for many years. Nobody forced her to do this. She made this decision after her mother died and she met the nuns from the order. Things loosened up a little for her eventually. At her age, anyway, she has most of her freedom back. It is interesting, though, to see how the isolated, meditative life most modern people would dread has benefited her. She is full of joy and youthful innocence and looks about thirty years younger than her real age. 'All the praying and hard work', she giggles with a very girly laughter that disarms me.

Martin accepts their invitation for dinner the next day. *What the fuck is he thinking?* Now I am sentenced to a dinner with them.

'I need a drink', I say vengefully and march Steve and Martin to the nearest pub where Steve has a Heineken, Martin his immortal Coca-Cola and I a *Cuba libre*. Steve leaves an abundant tip.

Steve knocks on my door while it is still dark.

'I'm sleeping', I yell, but he insists I get up. I put on my clothes and follow him to the roof deck on top of the hospice. The sun is just rising like a red ball coming out of the sky.

'Look', Steve whispers. 'That's Mount Hermon.'

In front of us is a mountain with its snow-covered peak in full view.

I am glad to know that these same vistas were available to Yeshua, that this is where he spent his adult years. There is no speculation. Here he definitely walked, taught and felt connected to the natural beauty of the world.

'You can't help but feel elated in Tiberias', I say as we go downstairs. We knock on Martin's door but he is already having breakfast in the dining room. I can't eat.

'Let's walk around the lake like he did', I say over coffee.

Martin and Steve look at me as if I am losing the plot.

'Like real pilgrims', I try again, without success.

'The car's already waiting outside', Steve says. 'I arranged it yesterday.'

We go outside. Steve sits in the driver's seat. I sit next to him.

'I feel like I could walk on water today', I exclaim.

No response.

'A perfect day for a pilgrimage', I try again.

'Drive before she convinces you otherwise', Martin orders Steve. 'I'm not walking anywhere. It would take a few days to walk around the Lake.'

The sky above the lake is blue and punctuated with delicate white clouds. The morning light makes the lake and the green hills around nearly translucent, as if they are floating above the ground. Everything seems weightless. My heart is weightless. My mind, for once, is not fixated on Melbourne and what is going to happen upon my return.

Our first stop is the Boat Museum.

Steve and Martin believe the boat there is the one Yeshua built and which he often sailed with his disciples. It has never occurred to me that Yeshua could sail on that beautiful lake. I can see him walking up and down the hills,—perhaps therefore talking about shepherds, I think naively—but not sailing as well. *Why not?*

Some of his closest disciples were fishermen. Certainly they had boats. This was how they earned their living. The mosaic in St Peter's Church in Tiberias showed a boat with two people in it. I was transfixed by that image; now I might be looking at the very same boat. The boat in question was discovered by two fishermen, Moshe and Yuval Lufan, from Kibbutz Ginosar. Its discovery caused lots of commotion because the boat had been built in the first century, and was significant for Jewish history as it could have been used during the Jewish rebellion against the Romans. The discovery was even more exciting for Christians, as it could have been the boat which Yeshua sailed with his disciples. The boat is made of twelve types of wood and is apparently an example of great craftsmanship. It was built with love. Steve tells me *The Urantia Book* mentions that Yeshua built a boat and used different types of wood to make it strong and graceful. I don't know what is true, but it is easy to believe that the boat was built by Yeshua's loving hands.

> In my soul, in my soul's eyes, I can see Yeshua building the boat. With his loving hands. In full Presence. His disciples standing around him, helping him, passing him tools, but mostly just being there, witnessing the Teacher. *How fully Present he is*, they think as they watch him, watch his hands touching the wood of the boat as if he were caressing it—as if the boat was a child of God, the most precious being on Earth, the first being on Earth. Blessed. They watch him and feel his Presence. They feel the Presence of Something. Is it the Presence of the 'Father' he is talking about? They do not know, but the Presence is there in his every move, in his every breath—in every word he says or does not say. He just is. In a full Presence that brings tears to their eyes. Their Teacher so Present. My Peace I give. My Presence I give you, he says. It is in him and it passes through him to them. It passes into anyone who comes to meet him. The Presence. The Love. Yes, the Love. They breathe in relief. He loves them. He loves them with a Love no one has known before. He loves them with the Love he gives to everyone. Equally. His hands moving with enjoyment over the wood of the boat. He turns and looks at me with soft amusement in his eyes. He turns and looks at them with soft amusement in his eyes. Everything pauses. For a moment . . .

I leave the display and Steve and Martin behind, and walk to the small, empty pier on the lake.

'I'm by the Sea of Galilee, where he lived his best years', I keep thinking, still strangely elated. Years of grotesque images I don't understand of a crucified man-God, two millennia of theological discussions, of mindless prosecutions of heretics and the Jewish population, and the desperate attempts of the Church to control our perceptions of Yeshua and his teachings drop off me like unnecessary ballast. I feel even lighter as I walk onto the pier. Long, green grass grows in the marshy areas along the pier. It is completely empty.

'This was how Yeshua would have seen the shore from a boat', I think. *If he looked now, he could see me.* I feel a gentle pat on my arm, as if he is walking next to me. I don't dare turn around.

I hear a voice: *Sail with me.*

I freeze. It is useless to ask where the voice has come from.

Suddenly my heart bursts open. For a moment I am completely free, completely contented, completely at peace. And when the moment passes, I start crying as if I will never stop.

'What on earth does this mean', I think through tears, 'and what am I supposed to do now?'

In Capernaum Yeshua lived with the Zebedee family, built boats and taught in the White Synagogue. The architecture of the synagogue is beautiful. Against the background of the Sea of Galilee it floats like a white sail. I walk among the columns feeling peace and joy knowing he was happy here, surrounded by people who loved him, his days filled with work and meditation.

He taught here, in that synagogue, in these beautiful surroundings.

I sit by the ruined wall of the synagogue and write in my journal so the words won't get lost in time and impetuous personal feelings. Steve and Martin circle the synagogue waiting patiently for me. I can see him here: the young, brilliant man, the spiritual genius craving to share what he knows. The congregation listening, trying to grasp what he is saying, most of which seems too much for them to understand. Too many references to familiar things in an unfamiliar way. Too much beauty and truth requiring a higher understanding, a more sublime vision, requiring them to give up a lot of what they used to know as truth. *He speaks about the truth. Who is he to speak of truth? The young man of Nazareth? Why does he ask us to believe what is so difficult to believe?*

'I don't ask you to believe what is difficult to believe', he says. 'I ask you to surrender to the truth.'

'And what is the truth?' people ask themselves as they leave the synagogue. 'What is the truth and how do you know it?'

Capernaum is an old town, a fishing village from about 200 BCE. During Yeshua's times the Romans kept a small garrison here. The centurion of the garrison gained the respect of the Jewish population by helping with the building of the synagogue. Here Yeshua met his disciples—Simon (also known as Peter), Andrew, James, Matthew and John—and changed their lives forever. Here he also cured the centurion's favourite servant. For unknown reasons Capernaum was not a place of interest for the Crusaders or medieval pilgrims. The synagogue was buried and forgotten throughout the ages until the late nineteenth century, when an American, Edward Robinson, found the site which was later excavated by Charles Wilson. As with many other biblical places in the Holy Land, the Franciscans bought it and continued the excavations.

The sun is high in the sky, and Capernaum and its synagogue is filling up with tourists and tourist buses. I walk over to the modern church built over Simon/Peter's place. This is where the first disciple lived, fished, and carried out his family life and responsibilities until he met Yeshua. According to the Gospel of Matthew (4:19), 'Yeshua saw Peter and his brother throwing a net into the sea and he said to them, "Follow me and I will make you fishers of men", and they immediately left their nets and followed him.' The same happened when he saw two brothers, John and James Zebedee, as well as Matthew the tax collector. He simply said, 'Follow me', and they left everything.

What does that mean? I am wary of religious leaders and their demands on our lives. But I trust Yeshua. What does he want when he says that? What else does he want, other than that we be honest with ourselves, look beyond the narrow vision of our routine lives, open ourselves to a grander vision, see what we see from a divine perspective?

'The Kingdom of the Father is spread upon the earth and men do not see it', Yeshua proclaimed in the Gnostic Gospels. 'I want to show you how to see it.'

How can we see it? The message was lost in the dogmas, philosophies and theologies of the fathers of the Church and other ambitious men. The message got lost somewhere in the Church's synods, in the arguments about the scholastic details of Yeshua's teaching—details he would not recognise.

Where can you find it when it is so obscured?

Outside the church a young African Franciscan monk is chatting-up a small flock of South American nuns. They laugh sensually. Their white teeth contrast with their olive skins. The African monk is beaming with manly vitality. I could go up to him and kiss him. I could separate his white teeth with my tongue and feel his mouth on my mouth and feel his strong arms around me. I laugh at this Catholic girl fantasy. I laugh because it is so obvious, because it is so common, because it celebrates both the mystery of craving for God and the vitality of life. These two things shouldn't be divided. They should be one: God and life and the irresistible power of life.

'They should be one!' I want to scream.

The nuns continue to laugh seductively in their innocent, girly way. Their white skirts dance around them like butterfly cocoons ready to burst with the joy of life. I am happy for them.

'Be happy for them', I want to say to the crowd of bedazzled and tired tourists walking around with their Bibles. 'Be happy for them because they are made of life, they are made of spirit, because the spirit and life are one and the same.'

Change your vision. Change your vision.

A shock of bougainvilleas, flamenco red, purple, golden and pink with tiger yellow eyes, jump at me outside the synagogue. Down the hills I notice mango orchards and I smile. *He ate the mangoes.* Yeshua ate the mangoes. He took their skin off delicately, precisely, with his own fingers. The smell of mangoes entered his nostrils and penetrated his senses with delight. He was a young man celebrating life, celebrating creation. The juice fell on his chin and he licked it with his tongue.

He saw the bougainvilleas. A young man pausing for a moment to see how feminine their flowers were. Here among the exploding bougainvilleas, by the mango trees, he made his disciples jealous when he kissed Mary Magdalene.

'Why does he love her more than us?' they whined like children. 'Why does he kiss that woman? Teacher! Teacher? Who are you?'

Bethsaida is the next stop, near Capernaum. Steve and Martin tell me there are two Bethsaidas: Bethsaida Proper and Bethsaida Julias. They take me to Bethsaida Julias to show me it could not have been the place where the fishermen-disciples anchored their boats. It is high on the hill above the lake. No boat could anchor here. They calculate by minute descriptions from the Bible and *The Urantia Book* that Bethsaida Proper is very close by. They point at the spot. According to tradition, Yeshua performed many of his miracles in the general area of Bethsaida—among them the feeding of the multitudes. I'm getting lost in all the places and details, but vaguely remember his miracle of feeding the hungry. He fed them out of compassion and his love multiplied the food so it was enough for everybody. When they all came back the next day, he refused to satisfy their curiosity because this time they returned not out of hunger but for a show of magic.

'Show us, Teacher, show us, how you can multiply food so we don't have to do anything to be fed.'

He smiled at them indulgently and told them to go away.

We stop at a small German church in Tabgha where, according to tradition, the feeding of the multitudes took place. The plaque on the church indicates that the site was visited by Egeria, another early medieval woman pilgrim. She followed the trail of the Empress Helena about sixty years later (at the end of the fourth century), and travelled through the Holy Land as a pilgrim. There is an interesting story about the accounts of her pilgrimage: as she travelled through the Holy Land, she sent letters to her nuns in Spain. Fragments of the letters were found copied in the Monte Cassino monastery in Italy in the eleventh and twelfth centuries. Specialists in medieval manuscripts are like highly skilled detectives, looking for records of the same documents in different forms in several countries, wondering what historical chance makes some documents survive and others disappear without a trace. We know, for example, that Plato's notes were lost during the Middle Ages, but his dialogues survived. We also know that Aristotle's dialogues perished, but his notes survived. What kind of historical accident enabled Egeria's account to survive the turbulent centuries of European history? In this church she is commemorated on a plaque as a woman-pilgrim of the fourth century.

We move on and stop at another small church called the Church of Peter's Primacy. The church was built on the site of a much older chapel erected in the fourth century; this was destroyed and new churches were built in its place, depending on who happened to be in power in the Holy Land. I walk down the set of stairs leading right to the edge of the stony beach and sit on a rock by the water. Somewhere here, as the waves wash against the beach, Yeshua met his disheartened disciples after his crucifixion. They came here because he had instructed them to do so before his ordeal, and/or perhaps because Mary Magdalene told them so. The disciples were still upset that she had seen him first after the resurrection. She saw Yeshua and he spoke with her—but he didn't talk to them. They were anxiously waiting for him, traumatised by his death, uncertain of his resurrection, doubting Mary Magdalene's report, but hoping she was telling the truth. They went fishing, as they were hungry. But they were too dispirited to catch any fish, and they returned to the beach empty-handed. Yeshua called to them from the sand, casually, almost humorously: 'Children, have you any fish?'

'No', they answered, so he told them where to catch the fish.

'It is the Teacher!' one of them yelled. 'It is the Teacher!'

They landed on the beach and greeted him, marvelling at his presence there.

'Teacher! You are here!'

'Where was your faith?' Yeshua smiled softly. 'Where was your faith, children?'

Over a fire on the beach, they sat around him and cooked the fish together while he spoke to them.

Then Yeshua turned to Simon/Peter and asked, 'Do you love me, Peter?'

While reading the many accounts of the resurrection, I always wondered why his closest disciples didn't recognise him at first. Was it the shock? Was his body transformed? Did he come to them as a spirit? Or did he speak to them from their inner selves?

Talk to me, Teacher.

On the way back to Tiberias (we have completed Yeshua's tour of the Sea of Galilee) Martin wants to stop at the Mount of Beatitudes. Somewhere in the area Yeshua gave one of his most important sermons—or at least this is what tradition and the official gospels claim. This time nobody is claiming they know where it happened exactly. This is more a place of commemoration. A Byzantine chapel was built here in the fourth century. Just before the Second World War, a Franciscan nun built a new chapel overlooking the plains of Gennesaret: a charming, garden-like place with blossoming roses and armies of hungry bees. Martin walks around carrying around a seemingly uninteresting set of papers and notes. He drops them on the grass of the garden. I come up and help him gather them. Some are old, yellowish pieces of paper with notes on them, some are serviettes with his unreadable handwriting.

'What a mess', I joke.

'It's not a mess', Martin defends himself seriously as he rearranges the papers in a highly complicated pile. 'This is the sophisticated filing system which the whole trip is based on. Dates of Steve's early trips and dates of my trips with him, the measurements of the tomb, the conversations with the sisters in the Nazareth and all our ideas as presented for the lawyers, and much more.'

Steve disappears into a cafe next to a gift shop, only to come back five minutes later with two espressos and grapes for us and a Coke for Martin.

I inhale the smell of proper coffee—my first coffee from an espresso machine since Jerusalem—and pass the grapes to Martin, but he declines. 'Too healthy for me. They'd upset my digestive system.'

Steve is ready to go and urges us towards the car. 'Any other requests?'

Yes, there is another request, this time from me. We stop at the breathtaking Greek Orthodox church I noticed on our way to Capernaum. Its pure pink domes exude an inviting, feminine energy. A small gravel path there leads to a rustic vegetable garden and a church. Two workmen are standing on ladders trying to fix loose tiles on the roof. They ignore our presence as if we are invisible. The church doors are locked. On the path to the stony beach stands a heavy wooden table that could feed a dozen people, but it is empty now.

Martin finds an old, broken signpost in English: *The Church of Mary Magdalene.*

It makes sense. The place carries a similar feeling to the Church of Mary Magdalene in Jerusalem, except that this one is even more beautiful. Joyful and natural.

'I could stay here, read and write, secluded from everything', I think, as if complete seclusion was possible. Would it take me away from my mind, from my ambitions and turbulent affairs with men? All my attachments and dreams?

Steve and Martin are already in the car. I jump in, glad they allow me so much space, allow me to be with this place by myself. Steve has been here twice before and a third time with Martin; they cherished the time they spent one-on-one with the places where Yeshua lived. It is my time now and they both understand.

Just before Tiberias we pass by Magdala, the place where Mary Magdalene came from and the place which gave her her biblical name: Mary of Magdala or Mary Magdalene. I don't ask them to stop. It is a quiet, residential area, with modern houses and garages, and fenced gardens. I won't find her here in that suburban development. She doesn't belong here. Neither do I.

Through the sublime vistas of the Sea of Galilee we approach Tiberias. The streets around the Casa Nova are sealed. There is no sign of the usual nightlife on the main strip. A serious-looking young man from the Israeli army tells us that an unclaimed bag has been found in one of the cafes and they are checking whether a bomb has been planted there by terrorists. In his seriousness he believes this possibility. In his reality this happens all the time. We walk off back to the beach and our lodgings.

'I'd like to go to Acre', I mention the next day over breakfast.

'Done!' Steve says, and Martin instantly goes to his room to pack.

LAST DAYS

A cre (or *Akko* in Hebrew, *Akka* in Arabic), is like a beautiful, mysterious woman with a past. Many great men of all faiths have died for her. You don't really know where she lives and with whom, because many claim her. You only know stories about her. To know her you need to make an effort, to study history books, the chronicles of her triumphs and tragedies. Travel agents don't recommend her. She has no resorts; a medieval beauty abandoned by time. She remained the last fortress faithful to the Crusaders and didn't fall until 1291.

Acre is still essentially a medieval town with an even older history. For me, the Crusader past is captivating. I have a feeling that even now I wouldn't be able to say no to a handsome warrior with a cause. The history of the Crusades is confusing and tragic: a strange combination of facts, legends, alliances, greed and misdirected love for God. The first Crusade took place in 1099 with the conquest of Jerusalem, and a number of other Crusades followed after the Muslim world recovered from the shock of European invasion of its land.

There were some tragic Crusades, doomed by idealism. In 1212, the idea of a Children's Crusade was conceived. Several thousand children were sent unarmed to recover the Holy Land from the Muslims. Predictably, this was a disaster. The children left the port of Marseille on seven ships headed for the Holy Land. Two of the ships sank off the coast of Sardinia. The remaining five were attacked by a fleet of Muslim pirates and the children sold off to slavery in North Africa. There was also the ironic fourth Crusade which never reached the Holy Land. The Crusaders became stuck in Venice, where Venetian bankers demanded immediate payment for the ships they had built for the Crusaders. The Crusaders, short of cash from the start, became convinced in 1204 to instead attack the Christian capital of the Byzantine Empire, Constantinople. After pillaging that great city and forsaking any ideals of regaining the Holy Land, the Crusaders returned home with their trophies.

Among the high dramas of the Crusades, Acre was the loyal, indestructible fortress which lasted when all else was lost. There is a medieval romance about the city. The citadel, the Hospitallers' headquarters, has a masculine, warrior energy. The tour with rented headphones is confusing. I am bad with numbers, so being asked to follow numbers flamboyantly spread on walls without any logical order is a challenge for me.

'I'll stay in the car—I'm exhausted', Steve says, and leaves us after the tour of the citadel. Martin and I walk around the charming old town, which is much bigger than we originally thought. Big walls around the port made the fortress almost unconquerable. The southern Mediterranean Sea is surprisingly clear blue, and floats gently on the beaches outside the Crusader walls. It is late December in winter, but the weather is glorious, summery; there is no need for a jacket or long sleeves.

'It's sad', I say to Martin, 'that a place of such beauty and history is a sleepy, forgotten town'.

Acre begs for Bohemian cafes and picturesque artistic quarters: beautiful buildings with sophisticated metalwork on their balconies, windows and door handles could make dream-like studios overlooking the sea and the medieval walls. I can see them in the eye of my imagination: arched, clear windows facing a translucent blue sea simmering on the other side of the white medieval wall on which children and tourists walk, playing with the past, imagining past love stories, breathing in a salty sea full of more history than your imagination can contain. The city dreams itself, like a charmed princess lost in dreams of her past, or a child lost in a labyrinth of curiosities from an unleashed imagination. The city dreams its past so deeply, so sweetly, that it doesn't feel the present and can't imagine the future. The city is a lover adrift in the dream of a love affair which cannot happen. And if something at once so sweet and so terrifying leaves her life, why bother with the mundane upkeep, why put on makeup? The same thing won't happen twice. The pain is gone, the glory is gone; history has moved elsewhere and the conquests are long gone. Acre is like a charismatic older woman who will never be fully deciphered. Now and then she can share a secret from her past over a glass of wine in a cafe. Or maybe a melody from the past will bring something back to her heart—would she fancy sharing it with you?

We get lost in the winding medieval streets and bazaars until we reach the even poorer parts of the Old City, where young Palestinian men wander the streets wondering about the present and guessing a future that won't be dreamed by the city. They are lost too: they are walking in circles along with a city lost in an old dream.

Eventually the labyrinth opens up for the travellers, and Martin and I get to our point of destination: the white lighthouse. We find Steve sleeping in the car.

Yes, Acre is the ultimate femme fatale: she should be famous, showered with jewels and pursued by travellers. All she needs is a little bit of luck. All she needs is to get a real break. Her beauty is obvious; her past is yours to discover, full of courage, betrayal and lost hope. As you walk her streets, you just know she can be great again.

I sit on a bench overlooking the sea while Martin gets into the car. He is tired and sweating. He can feel his age, he says with forced ease. In slow, measured movements he attends to his ageing body, puts on some sunscreen and his black Australian hat, joking that, 'Here this hat makes me look like the wicked witch of down under'. I watch him as he checks his impenetrable 'filing system', making sure all things are done properly, with care.

'He likes to be useful', I catch myself thinking as I sit in the midday heat, 'organising big and little things in life with precision'.

Yes, I am sitting on a bench facing the Mediterranean Sea, that womb of western culture. I don't think I have any nationalistic sentimentalities left in me, for any country . . . but the Mediterranean Sea. I'm so lucky to be here.

Getting out of Acre is a traffic nightmare. I fall blissfully asleep as Steve and Martin manoeuvre out of the city streets. I wake up in Caesarea.

If Acre is a femme fatale, Caesarea is a sourpuss. The Herodian Harbour surrounded by Roman and medieval walls is everything Acre could be. The open boulevards by the sea are elegant and pampered. A long line of well-to-do people walk leisurely on the broad promenades. Nothing disturbs their day by the sea. Caesarea is the opposite of Acre. She believes she should be adored—and she is. She hides nothing; her treasures are well displayed. She is the woman who insists on her superiority, even if there is not much to prove it. She is the spoilt daughter, the coveted wife. She is the woman on the covers of magazines. We nestle in the Port Café. I sip on my cappuccino while Steve and Martin share a thin-crusted gourmet pizza.

'This is the life', Steve says, stretching like a contented cat.

A well-groomed, blond woman in a black power-suit manages the cafe.

'I could be like her,' I think, 'but somehow I don't have the inclination or the money.' There is a certain vital sensuality of the adventurer about me, and at times a sophisticated intelligence. I don't show any signs of that intelligence now. *Sigh.* All I have now are turbulent emotions and a messy personal life. Even as an adult woman with a Ph.D, I am nothing but an untamed child. My heart still carries lots of darkness, clouds of intense emotions, and an equally intense desire for freedom.

I look at our hostess, the perfect sourpuss—elegant and bored by her admirers.

I envy her a little because what she does works for her. She hasn't many talents, but those she has are well displayed. The designer outfit, the carefully bleached hair in a classy bun, and the perfectly manicured fingernails. *I wouldn't know how to paint my nails if my life depended on it!* She passes by our table. Both Steve and Martin look at her like beggars. Steve salivates over her as he pays the bill. He tries to chat her up, but she has other things on her mind. She accepts the money from him as if she couldn't be bothered and the immense tip couldn't possibly impress her. She has had better before. You see—it works! I want to come up to her skilfully made-up face and smack her with panache.

We drive to Jerusalem in darkness. I switch seats with Martin, whose arthritis plays up more when he's in the back seat. On the way to Jerusalem Steve tries to find his way through highways congested like intestines. At this time of the year night falls at five in the afternoon. Some time around eight we arrive at the Seven Arches and it feels like home.

In the morning I knock on my companions' doors: first Steve's, then Martin's. Their rooms are across from each other. They open their doors simultaneously, standing there with nothing on but their underwear and white T-shirts. They look like two sleepy boys, only Martin is older and shorter and Steve tall and youthful. I stand in the hallway looking at their hairy legs.

'What are we up to today?' I ask, full of morning vigour.

Steve rubs his eyes and Martin puts on his pants at the door. A cleaner passes by, pretending it is perfectly normal for a woman to talk to half-naked men in the hall.

'It's your call today', Steve says.

'I've got no plans, but I'm happy to go along', Martin mumbles.

'Okay. I'll make the call today', I say. 'We're going to Jericho!'

'Isn't it on the other side of the border? Don't we have to cross to the Palestinian side? Last time we weren't allowed to', Martin mumbles.

'We can ask at the lobby.' I'm fully determined to go to Jericho.

'Why Jericho?' Steve asks.

Why Jericho? I tell them how, as a teenager, I read *The Walls of Jericho* by a Scandinavian writer (Lundquist, I think). It told of a story based on the Old Testament about two Israelites sent by Joshua to conquer Jericho on Yahve's orders. Jericho was a Canaanite city, and the patriarchs brought the Israelite armies to begin the siege. Their minds were distracted by the fame of a certain courtesan in Jericho. Her name was *Rahab* (a 'harlot'), and she could please a man like no other. Under the darkness of night, two of the Israelites sneaked out from their camp and secretly entered the city. For the whole night they enjoyed the supreme pleasures of Rahab, both separately and all together. The palms of her hands and her feet were painted in bright colours, her skin was fragrant with exotic perfume, her vagina was like a paradise on earth. She was an artist at her trade. At dawn they left the city unnoticed by all but Yahve.

'What did I tell you?' Yahve stormed at them. 'Unworthy bastards.'

They begged forgiveness and apologised until Yahve was somewhat appeased.

They had done the wrong thing, they admitted, as they entered their army camp again—but Lord it was worth it! And as it was, Yahve granted Joshua a victory anyway. The beautiful Rahab helped them enter the city with their armies. Later she married Joshua himself. And why not? Bad girls always go with the winners.

St Augustine, my favourite tormented Saint, was appalled by the early Israelites. They were too earthy for him, too sexual. But I have always liked them. Okay, so they often had a complicated relationship with God. Who doesn't? And did they know how to live!

'So boys, are you ready for Jericho today?'

The receptionist at the Seven Arches tells us it is best to take a Palestinian driver on the way to Jericho. We pass by the Palestinian-Israeli border and show our passports. The Israeli border guards eye us with suspicion, check every detail of our passports, and ask a few questions of the Palestinian driver. He answers with forced politeness, defiantly.

One of the Israeli guards is a stunningly beautiful young woman with long blond hair and gorgeous blue eyes. She looks serious and impenetrable in uniform, with a machine gun slung on her shoulder. Steve turns to the Palestinian driver and says, 'There is nothing as sexy as a gorgeous chick in uniform'. The driver is not amused. He is too focused on helping us pass the border so he can earn his money for the day. They let us go and we move on to the Palestinian checkpoint. Our driver says something in Arabic in a friendly way, and they wave for us to pass without a check.

The old Jericho, *Tell es-Sultan*, is shockingly poor. It is so poor it feels dead. Even the way to Jericho leads through arid, barren hills nested with a few Palestinian households built of cardboard and not much better than the temporary cardboard structures the homeless build on the streets of Toronto or New York.

The people in Jericho are very kind. Young Palestinian men walk the streets with seemingly nothing to do. The same powerlessness and lack of purpose that other ghettos exude. There is a sense of defiance, desperation and abandonment running under the kindness. The fruit shops on the main street are the only happy and colourful oases in this place of greyness.

The site of ancient Jericho is in complete disrepair. Unprotected. Entry is only ten shekels.

'You should charge more', I tell the man at the entrance.

At the site there are none of the usual signs, explanations, artistic impressions or maps. Without prior knowledge of the site's archaeological importance, you could confuse it for an abandoned hole in the ground made by some disenchanted builder. But it is not so. It is not so. This place has a magnificent history. Jericho is probably the oldest known 'town': its earliest remains are from 7000 BCE, or over 9000 years ago, when people here lived a communal life. The archaeologists whined that the earliest inhabitants didn't have pottery—just simple hunting weapons and tools. But they *did* have some form of spirituality, creativity and artistic inspiration, as can be judged from the city's ancient graves. This is good enough for me. Jericho was abandoned several times, though more humans resettled here in the Bronze Age, about 3200 BCE, when its defensive walls were rebuilt sixteen times. Around 2000 BCE the city was overrun by nomadic tribes and resettled again.

The biblical conquest by Joshua, with the significant help of Rahab, must have occurred around 1190 BCE, but apparently there is no archaeological evidence for this. A number of Israelite kings ruled the city after that. In Roman times Jericho was known for its fragrant balsams and gardens. Mark Anthony offered one as a gift to Cleopatra.

The city's later history is the same as for so many places: the Byzantine Christians came; the Persians came and conquered the Christians; the Muslims came and conquered the Persians; the Crusaders came and conquered the Muslims; the Muslims conquered the Crusaders. The city then deteriorated for centuries, if not millennia. At the end of the nineteenth century the city began to breathe again. The archaeologists came and tried to retell its forgotten history.

The three of us walk around the excavations, moved by the poverty of the place and the complete lack of funds to preserve the site. A spunky new cable lift installed by an Austrian charity group takes us to Mount Temptation. According to the traditional scriptures, this was the place where Jesus was tempted by the devil. I don't care for the story—it sounds too ascetic and mythical for me. The mountain has many natural caves which for centuries attracted meditating hermits. A Greek Orthodox monastery hangs over the cliffs and caves like an adventurous sculpture.

The monastery is set up as a perfect meditation retreat. Small rooms overlook the precipice. All everyday worries about 'stuff' are absent. I can only imagine such freedom and lightness of being, where there is no ambition and no pressure to achieve and accumulate. The focus is on the inner life, not on outer dressings. Here I go off again with my fantasy of living in a beautiful, isolated monastery, writing a book. In a perfect peace which allows me to see things as they are.

We enter a room which tradition purports was built on the top of the cave where Yeshua meditated. A Greek Orthodox monk quietly appears. I am delighted to see him in his black robes with his long *Hesychast* beard. He must sense this, as he comes up to me, pointing to the icons and explaining their significance. I'm charmed and buy everything I can, including little pictures, reproductions of the icons—even booklets in Greek I can't read.

'This monastery looks like the old Greek-Byzantine monasteries in Cappadocia', I say. 'We need places like this for quiet meditation.'

His quietness suddenly disappears. He leans towards me, whispering with unexpected anger, 'This is all Greek. It was all ours, but they took it away from us. It should be Greek. To expel the sinners. Sinners everywhere'.

I move away from him slightly, creating distance between us. How is it possible that someone who has meditated for twenty-two years in the monastery's caves with their powerful history could be ascetic in such a wilful, stubborn way? His prayers and meditations haven't taught him compassion, nor have they given him a vision on unity; they've made him judgmental, caught in wars forged a long time ago.

By some strange coincidence, asceticism has become an integral part of spirituality in all traditional religions. It might be a necessary step towards a withdrawal from things and situations that distract us from the true purpose of our lives: to live in awareness we are a part of some grander plan and presence. It is a step towards saying no to things which blind us, promise happiness, but leave us drained and empty. It is a step away from our social conditioning which gives us values and sets goals for us which ultimately leave us asking, 'Is that all that there is to life?'

I can understand that this withdrawal could also bring a temporary negative judgment on the ways of a society obsessed with consumerism and the acquisition of material goods. That judgment and the feeling of anger and frustration with the world should be a temporary stage. The next stage should be love and compassion. All truly spiritual people exude love and compassion. They pass through the stage of withdrawal and asceticism to reach a much better, more joyful space of love and bliss. They don't see the rest of us as sinners and the world as sinful. They see us as full of light and potential for recovery from our confusion. They do *not* point fingers and judge.

I read a story once in the *Mahabharata* (a great Hindu epic) about two kings: one evil, one good. Lord Krishna asked the evil king what he saw around him. The evil king screamed in anger, 'I see evil and terrible, distorted souls everywhere, bent on doing evil!' Krishna then asked the good king, 'What do you see around you?' The good king responded, 'Oh! I see goodness and light everywhere and people who try to do good as best they can'.

Great spiritual teachings always ask us to cleanse our vision so that we can perceive things in their natural purity and light. 'The Kingdom of God is spread upon the earth, yet men do not see it', Yeshua said in the Gospel of Thomas.

'All you need is a little loving touch, baby', I want to say to the monk. 'All you need is love.' At that moment I feel like the proverbial temptress from *The Temptation of Anthony*. A holy monk in an isolated place tempted by a beautiful dancer. Maybe the dancer wasn't a beautiful temptress. Maybe the dancer was a wise soul, letting the Saint know he hadn't arrived yet. A perfect fantasy for a naughty girl with a religious bent.

The Alpine cable-lift takes us back to the *Tel Jericho* excavations. We drive through the empty streets. Young Palestinian men look at us with curiosity. Tourists must be sparse around here. We stop at the Seven Trees Restaurant, a spacious venue that could entertain over a hundred people. The tables are set in a luscious garden. And all empty. Not a single guest. A middle-aged Palestinian man comes out of nowhere and asks us to choose any table.

'This one?' I ask.

'It is a good table', he says cheerfully. 'Maybe you bring me luck and we will have a business here again.' He rubs his protruding belly with hopeful delight. 'No business for five years. Five years!'

Immediately he busies himself with giving orders to a young man behind the bar.

'Come out and clean the tables in the garden!' he yells at him. He pushes the chairs away from our table and like a *basha* roars with great vigour an invitation for us to sit down.

As he and the younger men attend to us, I can see how easily this place could be transformed into a land of plenty. Jericho was once called the City of Palms: a city of fragrant oils worthy of Cleopatra, a city where gardens were always in full blossom and trees were heavy with fruit.

'You should be full with guests from all around the world', I say to him.

'I know', he exclaims in a deep, powerful voice.

'Your gardens should be beaming with people eating the best food.'

'I know', he exclaims even more cheerfully.

'What happened to the fountain?' Steve points to a large fountain in the middle of the garden. Dry.

'No water. Out of order. But we will fix it again. Tell people to come here.' Then he yells in the direction of the invisible kitchen: 'Bring our best food for our best guests'.

'Do you have any children?' Martin smiles at the man, like one family man recognising another.

'Oh yes', the man laughs. 'Lots of children.'

'I have seven', Martin says. 'And you?'

'Thirteen', the man caresses his belly with contentment. 'Thirteen children and thirty-five grandchildren. The only problem', he leans over our table, 'is that I can't remember their names. My wife will kill me if you tell her'.

He becomes serious when he says, 'Tell people that there are nice people here who want to live, have children and live safely. We don't support any terrorists. We are caught between the government and the terrorists. We are good people. And we have good food if you come.'

We leave Jericho and drive off to the Dead Sea, passing by arid, infertile hills. The Dead Sea among them. In my imagination it becomes a place where the gods walk when they are angry with humans. Or a place where humans come if they want to repent, ready to face the gods' rage. It is a place where John the Baptist and other ascetically inclined men and women lived. We are heading towards Ein Gedi where John the Baptist had his headquarters. And where King David lived in exile. The Dead Sea Scrolls were discovered in 1947 in the Ein Gedi caves. But we never make it there.

The roads are deserted. Everywhere we see empty army bunkers and abandoned military barracks. Now and then we see small rocks covered in black mud called 'beaches'. On the tiny strips of beaches middle-aged men and women cheerfully smother themselves in black mud and bake in the sun. Or else they hop into the sea, gather the black mud in small buckets and run back to their beach chairs, as if they have found the elixir of youth and immortality. The mud is said to have rejuvenating qualities for those who choose to believe. There is something grotesque in the picture: the arid, ascetic land, the lifeless sea devoid of beauty, and the desperate middle-aged couples looking for instant youth. I don't know which is worse: this or Hollywood plastic surgeons.

We stop at some sort of resort. The wire fence blocks the entrance to the beach. Loud Latin music pours through the fence and into the desert. Behind the fence young, barely dressed women are dancing salsa with much older men who, by any standards, are past their sexual prime. The young women seem unusually happy with the whole arrangement as they dance with the skinny-legged old men, whose swollen guts hang above their knees as they try to keep up with their partners. It definitely is some kind of oasis, but quite different from what Ein Gedi once was. A woman in her early fifties comes up to us, shoots us an amusing glance.

'You need to pay to get in here', she says in a relaxed, lazy way. She is dressed in an exotic nomadic robe, deep blue with silver trimmings. Her eyes are heavily accentuated by thick black eye liner, making her eyelids appear sleepy and sensual.

'I don't like this place', Steve decides, as if she isn't there.

The woman smiles indulgently and says, 'Your choice'.

'That's quite a resort', Martin says, amused.

I look at the woman, still standing at the gates of the fenced-off part of the beach, regal in her silvery robes and with the attitude of a woman who has seen many things in her life—things 'good' girls aren't privileged to see. There is an ancient glory about her, some primal power which could seduce the greatest among men. A long time ago Joshua at the walls of Jericho couldn't have resisted her charms.

'Rahab', I think admiringly as we drive off.

It feels like we are leaving our home in Jerusalem, the Seven Arches Hotel. Steve has booked us in for a night of luxury at the American Colony Hotel. The hotel is what is left of what was once a Christian colony in Jerusalem. Separate to the sectarian colonies, it was committed to peace and the sharing of different traditions. The Spafford Family left Chicago in 1881 to establish a self-sufficient colony in Jerusalem. Their decision to settle in Jerusalem came after a number of personal tragedies struck them in America. Destiny is sometimes a mysterious thing. Something awful has to happen before we find our goals and our true selves.

This is what happened to the Spaffords: the loss of property, the death of children, religious persecution. Upon their arrival in Jerusalem their lives took on a different dimension. They created a peaceful enclave in the middle of the warring city, an enclave which was respected by the Jewish and Islamic populations alike. Now it is a luxurious hotel, with a grand courtyard, fountains, red and pink bougainvilleas blossoming in colourful pots, and small round tables with artistic ceramic tops tempting you to sit down, order a coffee and write in your journal.

I get a corner room, number 209, overlooking a minaret. My imagination speaks to me again in a voice of desire for my own place. I have never wanted a suburban house or the so-called stabilisation everyone around me seeks. But I have longed for a place where I can camp long enough to write and experience what is needed to be experienced. I have longed for a beautiful place that inspires my senses, fires up my imagination, satisfies my curious soul. So I dream again about staying in this beautiful room forever and writing my book. I snap out of the fantasy. Writing is about writing. Looking for a perfect setting to write is a form of escapism from . . . writing.

'Do what you need to do now. Do the best you can do under the circumstances', I repeat to myself what I have learned from

191

studying the Hindu *Gita*. I wish my own traditions would give me such good guidance, would teach me about empowerment, would give me insights into my own being, my place in the world and my connection with God. Instead they tell me I am a sinner, born so because two mythical people I have never met ate an apple. If this isn't enough, if I don't do what my church tells me to do, I will burn in eternal fires. Well, I feel like telling the Church, you can keep that religion to yourself. I feel rebellious as I collapse on the white bed in a fury.

The phone is ringing. 'Are you ready? We're waiting in the lobby.'

I jump out of bed. It is time for our meeting with Shmuel Yaari.

The taxi driver gets lost. He is a Palestinian, he explains, and normally he doesn't go to the Jewish part of modern Jerusalem. 'I have never been here', he says. 'My first time on this side.'

Eventually we find Shmuel Yaari's flat. He welcomes us with a pot of tea and an apple cake made by his wife. She is not there, is spending time with friends on a farm.

'Do you think this is a social meeting?' I ask Steve.

He shrugs. 'Who knows?'

Shmuel asks us to sit around a coffee table. 'Here is another one of my books', he says, passing a book *Jerusalem, Man and Stone* to me.

I take it like a precious gift. 'Twentieth edition? That's very impressive.'

He nods and points at the delicate tea cups and the apple cake on the table. 'Help yourselves.'

We sit like children visiting an old auntie, not sure what to expect, when the bell rings and Oren appears at the door. Aah! So it *is* a business meeting. I relax, but Steve and Martin become tense. There will be news about the tomb.

Shmuel pours some tea and offers the cake to Oren, who greedily takes a slice. I like Oren very much: an intelligent young man without any prejudice towards the three mad Aussies who claim they may have found the tomb of Yeshua. In his world Christians are nothing but trouble, but he is bigger than that. He appreciates our commitment and is too well-educated to judge us according to his own standards.

'I have something for you', Oren says. 'I collected some material at the site. Didn't sleep until two in the morning.'

'You must be tired', I say, playing mother.

'No, no! Jacob told me he had to work very hard to get where he is and I listen to everything he says.'

Shmuel checks whether we are all full of cake and tea.

'I can confirm', he begins, 'that it probably is a first-century tomb from the Second Temple period'. He looks for the effect. I grin like an idiot. Steve stares at Yaari and Martin exclaims victoriously, 'Aha!'

'This is great news', Oren says, genuinely happy. 'This is really great news.'

'The first thing you should do is either buy the land or lease it. Can they lease the land?' He turns to Oren.

'Sometimes you can get permission to lease for a hundred years, but it is safer to buy.'

'Maybe safer, but dearer', Shmuel replies.

'I'll lease it if necessary, but I'd prefer to buy', Steve says. 'To protect the site.'

'The land in question might be the property of a *waqf*. If it is, the Muslims will probably build a mosque there. The other possibility is that it is a family *waqf* which is subdivided into many plots as an inheritance.'

'I have a list of names who might—I stress *might*—own the land.' Oren passes the list to Steve.

Steve puts on his John Lennon glasses and reads the list from Oren. I try to peek over Steve's arm, but can't see what is on the list.

'So thirty people own the land? If need be I'll go and talk to each and every one of them about the project. I'll tell them I come in peace.'

'That's good', Oren says with disbelief.

'Will you tell them we think it's Jesus' tomb?' Martin can't help himself.

Shmuel smiles. 'I would not advertise that possibility as yet. The best thing is to secure the land privately and, when ready, to begin proper excavations. I would suggest a non-Catholic archaeologist so there will not be a conflict of interest. A Catholic archaeologist might object to the whole thing.'

We all agree.

'The best option, I believe', he continues, 'is a cooperation between a western archaeologist connected to an established university and someone from the Antiquities here. It appears to be a typical first-century tomb, I can guarantee you that. But whether it is Jesus' tomb, you may never be able to prove or know'.

He takes the book back from me and opens it at a page showing the plan of the tomb in the Holy Sepulchre. 'I checked this once more. The tomb in the Holy Sepulchre could be the tomb, although I doubt it.'

'What do you mean, it could be the tomb?' I ask. 'The Holy Sepulchre is within the city walls and no burials were allowed within the city.'

He nods. 'There is some discussion going on as to whether or not that part of the city wall was moved. The walls were moved many times throughout history. So the Holy Sepulchre might or might not contain the tomb. It is certain, though, that the

Garden Tomb discovered by the English is not Jesus' tomb. It is too old. It was built in an earlier era of the First Temple period. Too old to be his tomb.'

Oren's mobile rings. 'Jacob?'

We all wait for him to finish. I pick up the book from Shmuel and use it as support to write down what has been said.

'I would like to work with you,' Shmuel offers, 'but you also need help either from Europe or America. It would be good if you could convince some established archaeologist and a biblical scholar to work with us'.

'I just spoke to Jacob'. Oren interrupts. 'There is more news. The list of thirty owners of the *waqf* that Steve has now is not correct.'

Steve puts the list down and looks at Oren expectantly.

'Jacob told me that the land doesn't belong to the *waqf* anymore.'

'So what are we going to do?' Steve asks.

'This might be good news', Oren grins. 'We might be able to buy the land easier. The land might have one owner. I want to see the site again. Is it safe on that side of the city?'

'It's safe', Steve assures him.

Oren is not convinced, so Steve invites him to go with us in a taxi.

I put away my journal. Things are moving fast. Too fast for me to process. I am suddenly overwhelmed by the possibility that it could be *the* tomb. I want to go to the American Colony and have a nice dinner and a glass of wine. I want something less complicated and less divine. Ideally, to make love to a dark, handsome stranger—or something equally as dumb. To forget, to escape the vortex in my soul. My capacity for the divine is rapidly diminishing.

—◦◦◦◦◦◦—

Our last day in Jerusalem. Martin wants to estimate and measure the distance from the Damascus Gate the women who went with Mary Magdalene to visit Yeshua's tomb had to cover. That, he tells us, will help him calculate the place of crucifixion. He isn't satisfied with the Holy Sepulchre at all, and doesn't believe General Gordon's 'Hill of the Skull' is correct either.

'Let's visit the places we haven't had time to see earlier', I propose.

We walk from the American Colony Hotel to Gethsemane or, as it is known now, the Church of All Nations. It strikes us as new and very recently built—or rebuilt, I guess, as nothing in this city has been built one time only. This is the great romance I have with ancient cities like Jerusalem. Inevitably you face something grander than yourself. You learn admiration, awe. It offers a scale against which you can measure yourself and your life, your material concerns. So what about that mortgage you are worrying yourself to death about? What about the promotion you didn't get—or, ironically in my life—that job you can't get? What about that romance which consumes you, that man you can't stop thinking about, or your own hopes for greatness? *This* is greatness! Here around you, under your feet and on all sides, wherever your eyes can reach . . . *here* is greatness. You walk the streets where people have loved, suffered, lost and gained for thousands of years . . . and you think you have problems?

The Crusaders savaged the city out of their mad lust for God and glory. Yeshua—call him a God, Jesus, a great being— met his final hours here in agony. Solomon had his temple here; Muhammad went to heaven here; people are still fighting the raging fire of passion for God. And you worry about that job, about that payment, about that man who has consumed years of your life and heart? What a great relief to be aware of this. What a relief to see things in perspective. To see yourself from the perspective of the great drama of life. The city makes you so poignantly aware that this is what it is—a great drama. Only ancient cities have it. Modern cities, with their suburbs and skyscrapers and ambition and narcissism, are flat. They have no perspective. You just run. If you're not in the race, then you wish you were, because there are only two places to be: a part of the maddening, meaningless run after STUFF, or being out of the run and feeling bad about it. Ancient cities teach you things, and they have energy that carries you to deeper understanding.

Gethsemane, just like any other place in Jerusalem, symbolises a state of the human psyche. Gethsemane is about betrayal and surrender at the same time. Yeshua sat here by himself, waiting in agony, knowing he would be betrayed by one of his closest disciples. He was aware of what was ahead of him. The biblical text usually associated with this moment comes from Matthew (26:39): 'My Father, if it is possible, let this cup pass from me: nevertheless not as I will, but as You will.' All the gospels, the Bible and the gnostic sources, agree that Yeshua felt fear in knowing what was awaiting him, and all these books stress the humanness of his state. All the sources also tell the same story.

In the evening before his arrest, Yeshua prayed in agony on the stone in Gethsemane. He asked the disciples who camped with him to watch over him, but they repeatedly fell asleep. This was the moment he recognised how alone he was in his ordeal. In moments of great trials, we are asked to face them alone. *The Urantia Book* talks about Yeshua experiencing 'private loneliness' and 'indescribable heaviness'.

He spent the next day in the olive grove nearby, which, as tradition says, was the place of the present olive grove by the church.

Meanwhile, Judas arranged for the betrayal in the city. He asked to be accompanied by soldiers, but arrived ahead of them. He told the soldiers he would kiss Yeshua on his arrival so they would know whom to arrest. As planned, he came up to Yeshua and kissed him. Seconds later the soldiers arrested Yeshua.

Every truly great story that survives time carries something with it that lives in us. This story is about the inevitability of suffering. When you are in Gethsemane, when you walk among the thousand-year-old olive trees you think, 'He too walked in this olive grove. He sat here and cried, overwhelmed by the consequences of his life and, finally surrendered to what was the fulfilment of his destiny'. You can't be untouched by that.

A sign on the plaque under one of the olive trees in the grove says (as I remember it):

> In deepest night and agony you said these words
> of trust and surrender. In love and gratitude I want to
> say in times of fear and distress, 'My Father, I do not
> understand You, but I trust you'.

These are powerful words. Words of surrender to a higher will. These were difficult words for me, as I had been trained to believe in the triumph of personal will, in the achievements that come from that. I had become very attached to these achievements and had given myself over to them. Inevitably, though, they hadn't been enough. All energy had left me. It felt like my life had left me and the fruits of my work hadn't yet appeared. I had found myself unemployed with disintegrating relationships. My whole being had disintegrated as well.

But it had prompted a deeper search. If what you wanted so much wasn't given to you, you had to inquire why. *Why?*

From Hinduism and mystics of all traditions I learned that the loss of what we know as our 'self' is a positive thing and a necessary step in a spiritual evolution. An evolution to the Self: more original, more divine—truer than the self. In western traditions we call it the 'soul.' Master Eckhart, a great twelfth-century German mystic, said, 'If we do not get the spiritual benefits of this birth, then that is because we are not content to allow God to act in us. We obstruct Him with our notions of self and the determination to cling to nothingness'. These were tough words. The determination to cling to nothingness. This meant that everything we considered important in our lives and struggled and worked so hard to accomplish was really nothingness. Was this fair? I didn't think it was wise to take this literally. Naturally, these things—usually career and relationships—were important, and even necessary, for our psychological health, but what that text was saying was that there was a greater vision of ourselves, and we needed to tap into that too. I had no choice but to ask myself: 'What is a vision of myself I don't see? What is the higher vision?' Not in the sense of a higher, better accomplishment, but a more integrative vision which is not only about my career, my relationships and my happiness. What is this greater vision? 'Father, I do not understand you but I trust you.'

Hmm. I sit quietly in the grove as Steve and Martin talk to an old Franciscan friar who is opening the doors to the church.

I insist we go through the Davidson Centre, where the blocked-off gates to the Holy of the Holies stand. These are the gates to the Holiest of Jewish Temples and the Golden Mosque of the Muslims. 'I need to check what's there', I say with sudden conviction.

Steve buys the tickets and we all go through the excavations to the blocked-off gates. I press my body against the wall and feel the divine vortex, the pulsation of the Energy.

'Can you feel it?' I ask Steve, who clings to the gates with his body.

'This is some energy field', he says, as if in a daze. 'This is some energy field.'

Martin comes up and tries to do the same. 'I can't feel anything, you new-age freaks.'

But I can feel he is upset, feels that God loves 'freaks' more than IT programmers. As if to confirm it, I hear Martin complain like a child, 'I'd like to feel it too'.

'This stuff really vibrates', Steve says. He can't get over the experience.

'It's a divine vortex', I say. 'Whatever it is, whoever claims it, It's alive with some powerful energy.'

'Oh shut up!'

Martin orders us to the exit and through the Lion's Gate to our cafe between the Austrian House and the corner of the Fifth Station. The cafe, which is usually empty, is full now. The young Palestinian man who runs the cafe welcomes us with open arms.

'Huh. Here you are. You brought me good business. No one used to come here, and now look.'

Martin laughs that we bring good business everywhere we go. The young man offers us drinks and pistachio cakes with honey. 'On me', he says. 'It is on me.'

At the Damascus Gate Martin gets serious again and makes his calculations, discussing them with Steve. 'They need that', I think. They need that certainty, that precision. They have the need to correct things. I'm not here to correct anything, to claim anything. The only correction I need to make is the one to my relationship with Yeshua, with what I was taught, with what corrupted that relationship and made it impossible.

I walk into two beautiful churches: the Basilica of St Stephen and the Cathedral of St George. St Stephen's is a charming French church built on the spot of a much earlier church from 431 CE by Juvenal, Bishop of Jerusalem. The Empress Eudacia provided the funds and support. A few years later Cyril, the infamous Bishop of Alexandria, came here to consecrate the church. Every inch of this land, I think, is scarred by the madness of devotion and destruction. Cyril is my personal enemy, as he ordered the killing of Hypatia, the great woman-philosopher in charge of the Library of Alexandria. The Basilica is in possession of French Dominicans. You can give one thing to the French: they have good taste in art. I recognise Thomas Aquinas, Catherine of Sienna and Jerome on their frescos. There is also a beautiful painting of Mary Magdalene, shown in the French tradition as a woman with long red hair, holding a jar with ointments, which, according to tradition, she poured on Yeshua.

The Cathedral of St George next door is very different in ambiance, very English. I recognise the crosses of the Templars, the Crusader Order of St John's, everywhere. They were dedicated to the Church by the Order. I thought they all died. After the fall of Acre they moved first to Rhodes, then to Malta. But apparently not. Not in Jerusalem at least, where ancient grudges and loyalties are preserved with great reverence and madness. On the wall to the left at the entrance of the church a painting catches my attention: Yeshua's crucifixion and resurrection. On the painting he is transformed by light— there is no cross; only a passing to the Light.

Steve and Martin find me there.

'We think the crucifixion took place where the white nuns have a convent across the street. Or more precisely, in their garden', Steve says.

'Across the street from here?' I ask.

'Yes!' They are in unison, on a mission again.

'We can't get in there', Martin says. 'The gate's closed.'

We cross the street. The doors to the convent are locked. I knock. Nothing happens. I knock again and the doors open. A middle-aged woman at the door asks, '*Oui?*'

My French suddenly returns and I chat with the woman, tell her we are pilgrims from Australia and would like to see the garden. The woman calls a nun who says in French that she doesn't have the authority to help us. She calls her superior. Another older nun appears and I discover once again that the only way to the French heart is to speak French and, sure enough, the nun says that *oui, bien sur*, we can see the garden, which is *tres joli*.

The gates to the garden open and we go in. The garden is cultivated with love. There is no one there but the three of us and an old Palestinian gardener. As if to indulge our need for closure, a tall cactus in the shape of a cross dominates the garden.

Let's say it did happen here, in this place. Why not? It is as close an approximation to the Holy Sepulchre, or even closer. It doesn't have the madness of fanaticism that the

Holy Sepulchre does, or the same overexposure of a tourist attraction. This place is peaceful. And quiet. This place can convey the experience of what happened two thousand years ago. Let's try. I close my eyes and I feel no horror. I remember what Swamiji told me about Yeshua transcending, suffering, through spiritual triumph. Sometimes things happen to us that we don't understand. That we may never understand. Painful things. Suffering. And sometimes the only choice we have is whether we become bitter because of the pain or whether we cross to the Light and let those experiences transform us and help us become the Light. I look at the cross and feel no fear, no pain. I feel peace in my heart. Peace and acceptance. So the cross happened. It was supposed to happen, so it did. What is left is Peace. *My Peace I give you.*

It is all gone, Teacher. It is all gone. All I feel is the passion of Life. All I feel is pain among the moments of joy.

He smiles: *This is the best moment to feel Peace.*

'In the midst of pain and confusion?' I ask.

In this moment. This is the very moment to feel the Peace. My Peace I give you. My Peace I give you.

I'm not used to this Peace. I'm used to intensity and passion. I'm used to questioning what I am told is the truth, and I'm used to being rebellious. I'm not used to this Peace. I'm not used to this feeling of acceptance. But I want to hold it for a moment so that when I'm back to my turmoil I can return to this Peace. Remember it. Hold it.

I am not used to this Peace.

EPILOGUE

Upon our return to Melbourne, Steve held many teleconferences with the lawyers in Tel Aviv. He offered to build a garden free of charge on the property, A place of beauty so people might hesitate before tearing it down. It would give the tomb some protection.

Jacob thought this was a good idea. He knew the Lord Mayor of Jerusalem. The Mayor believed the council could approach the *waqf* on Steve's behalf and say, 'There's a generous donor who would like to build a garden on that land, obligation free'.

Jacob advised Steve that the Trust had to be prepared to appoint a landscape architecture company, preferably one well known in Jerusalem, so he could go to the council with a plan of the garden.

On Steve's next trip to Jerusalem in 2006, we would learn that twenty years earlier, the city council had actually acquired the land with the intention of building a park. This was an extraordinary turn of events. The paperwork had been sitting in the council chambers and everybody, more or less, had forgotten about it. Everyone assumed it was still *waqf* land, even though it had already been declared parkland after the 1967 war. Suddenly there was a whole new plan on the table. The council didn't have to present this concept to the *waqf* and, because the council was interested in beautifying the city anyway for the benefit of the local people, it was decided that the garden was a fantastic idea. Steve thought that a garden was a simple solution to a complex problem and a gift to the people of Jerusalem. Symbolically it was a beautiful thing to do. Jerusalem is a dry place. To build a garden there was symbolic of life, of growth, of beauty, of nature—a mini-garden of Eden. And what a place to build it on! Steve said he had a strong wish to visit the *waqf* trustees and ask them to join us in this venture of building a Peace Garden in the centre of Jerusalem. A garden for all religions. Everybody would be welcome and be able to relate to the idea. It would nurture innocence and good will in people. An act of good will that came from the heart unqualified—like an act of universal friendship.

In the meeting with the council Steve said, 'Everyone on the planet can share this. One way of knowing God is by doing good. The garden project is open to all people to visit and contribute. I hope it will remain a garden in perpetuity. This park is about friendship with God for all people, irrespective of their beliefs or religions. It's about the practice of friendship and good will'.

The council agreed that the plan was magnificent and in alignment with their wishes. The papers were prepared by our lawyers who, since our first mad trip to their office in Tel Aviv, had become our best supporters and friends. Tomb or no tomb, Jesus or no Jesus, the idea of a Peace Garden in the middle of Jerusalem meant to uplift people, to reconnect people of all faiths, appealed to Jacob.

When, early in 2011, I met Steve at the Orange Cafe on Chapel Street, he told me that in June 2010, the new Mayor of

Jerusalem, Nir Barkat, had signed an agreement enabling the garden project to proceed. I jumped off my seat when he very seriously said, 'Calm down. This isn't the whole story'. I looked at him, alarmed by the seriousness in his voice. 'A few weeks later, an unknown person, maybe a rogue land developer, decided to claim the land for himself. He started clearing the land, bulldozing the tomb in the process. The landscape architect that we'd hired for the garden went to survey the site and saw what was happening. He confronted the man and told him to stop as it was a municipal land designated for a garden. The landscape architect immediately informed the City Council. The developer, or whoever he was, disappeared and was never identified. I was devastated. For me, it was an act of mindless sacrilege. But nothing could be done. The tomb is gone, nothing's left to be excavated, but the Garden is approved and in the process of being designed.'

Steve was perched on the edge of his seat, as if ready to get up and fly to Jerusalem. He still had the same commitment and faith in the Garden—despite the destruction of the tomb. He found that many Jewish businessmen in Melbourne as well as Palestinian activists were interested in supporting the project. I had never known anyone who had the ability to uplift himself and people around him from their everyday states of mind. You just believed him, wanted to follow him in his adventures, if you had the inclination or courage. At the very least you wanted to hear about it and feel the thrill of something supernatural, bigger than the life you were living. Someone once called me 'single-minded' and I wanted to use the same description about Steve—but he wasn't single-minded. He was single-hearted. All his personality, the fullness of his heart, was dedicated to this project; there was no space for anything else in his life.

'When people want to do good', he said, 'they have to have total faith, total trust. And if we're presented with obstacles, we have to become masters at making good decisions'.

'Maybe', I added, 'it's for us to understand that it's all an integral part of the Grand Design. A privileged part that needs to retrace its steps to its Source and take responsibility for our presence here. In Peace. Without wasting energy on looking for the villains'.

I wanted to meet with Martin again and ask him what he thought about all that had happened since 2005, but he was away in Perth visiting his grandchildren.

I asked Steve, 'What drives you?'

He looked at me, and after a brief pause, responded, 'Desire for Oneness and Peace in the great madness of life. The tomb is gone but the Garden lives on'.

SELECTED REFERENCES

Books

Barks, C. (2005). *Rumi. The Book of Love*. HarperCollins, San Francisco.

Brown, P. (1969). *Augustine of Hippo*. University of California Press, Berkeley.

Kelly, J. N. D. (1975). *Jerome. His Life, Writings and Controversies*. Duckworth, London.

Kersten, H. (1994). *Jesus Lived in India: His Unknown Life Before and After Crucifixion*. Element, Rockport, Massachusetts.

Leloup. J. Y. (2002). *The Gospel of Mary Magdalene*. Inner Traditions, Rochester, Vermont.

Meyer, M. (1992). *The Gospel of Thomas. The Hidden Sayings of Jesus*. Harper Collins, San Francisco.

Shanks, H. and Witherton III, B. (2003). *The Brother of Jesus. The Dramatic Story and Meaning of the First Archaeological Link to Jesus and His Family.* Harper, San Francisco.

Shanks, H. (1995). *Jerusalem. An Archaeological Biography.* Random House, New York.

Spafford, V.B. (1988). *Our Jerusalem.* Ariel Publishing, Jerusalem.

The Urantia Book (1995). The Urantia Foundation, Chicago, Illinois.

DOCUMENTS

'The Friendship Garden of Jerusalem Trust. How the Grottoes of an Ancient Church were Discovered in the Convent of the 'Dames de Nazareth' at Nazareth in Galilee' by Father M. Lerpetre, O.F.M.

'Nazareth: A Century of History 1855-1955' by Father Senes.

'Where is the Tomb of Jesus? A Search Based on Information from *The Urantia Book*' by Stephen Shanahan and Martin McBurney.
'Friendship and a Discovery in Jerusalem' by Stephen Shanahan and Martin McBurney.

'In Israel' by Martin McBurney.

'Providence and the Secret of Nazareth' by Stephen Shanahan.

'Where are the Sites of Jesus' Death and Burial According to the Bible?' by Martin McBurney.

'Golgota and Calvary. The Elusive Tomb of Jesus of Nazareth.'

'Chronology of Trips to Israel' by Martin McBurney.

'The Comparison of Orthodox and Gnostic Schools of Thought' by Stephen Shanahan.

Extracts from Martin's emails to his family from Israel.

'The Excavations at Sisters of Nazareth' by Jean-Bernard Livio, S. J.

NOTES BY FATHER SENES

'Site Notes with Arculf's Description in the Year 670.'

'New Developments on the Life of St Joseph of Nazareth.'

'Nazareth—A Century of History, 1855-1955.'

'Excavations Carried Out in Nazareth at the "Sisters of Nazareth": The Adversaries'.

THE FRIENDSHIP GARDEN OF JERUSALEM PROJECT

The city of Jerusalem is more than 3000 years old and is sacred to the three great monotheistic religions. A few years ago two Australians were exploring this vibrant, fascinating city and came across a large block of neglected, barren land.

Soon after an idea was born: to create a beautiful and tranquil garden of world renown, supported by the people of the world in a spirit of goodwill, cooperation and inclusion.

By good fortune, the land in question—located some 800 metres north of the Old City—was gazetted as a public park. A proposal was presented to the Jerusalem Municipality, resulting in the Friendship Garden of Jerusalem Trust being established. The mandate of the Trust will be to create and maintain the Friendship Garden of Jerusalem.

The Trust is registered in Australia, is non-profit and has three Australian Trustees.

The Garden will be an exquisite exhibition of botanic beauty. As an international Friendship Garden, plants will be selected for it from around the globe. Plants of local, historic or special significance associated with the Holy Land will also be included.

The key design concepts for the Garden are harmony, sanctuary and silence—an oasis for the soul. Apart from an abundance of plants, there will extensive use of water—the very spirit of life itself.

Our fervent desire is that this Garden will, in perpetuity, be a gesture of goodwill from this generation to future generations.

Join us on this adventure as we transform this land.

www.friendshipgardenofjerusalem.com

Made in the USA
Monee, IL
10 September 2022

13715923R00135